C0-AVA-567

Powell Lectures on Philosophy
at Indiana University

W. HARRY JELLEMA, EDITOR

FOURTH SERIES

WARS OF
FAMILIES OF MINDS

FIRST SERIES

THE LASTING ELEMENTS OF INDIVIDUALISM

William Ernest Hocking

SECOND SERIES

IN THE SPIRIT OF WILLIAM JAMES

Ralph Barton Perry

THIRD SERIES

NATURALISM

James Bissett Pratt

FOURTH SERIES

WARS OF FAMILIES OF MINDS

William Lowe Bryan

WARS OF FAMILIES OF MINDS

BY

WILLIAM LOWE BRYAN

PRESIDENT EMERITUS AND
SOMETIME PROFESSOR OF PHILOSOPHY
AND PSYCHOLOGY, INDIANA UNIVERSITY

Published for Indiana University.

NEW HAVEN
YALE UNIVERSITY PRESS
London, Humphrey Milford, Oxford University Press.
1940

Printed in the United States of America

THE
MAHLON POWELL FOUNDATION

MAHLON POWELL—1842–1928
WABASH, INDIANA

Extract from the last Will and Testament of Mahlon Powell:

Having entertained a desire for many years to assist in the cause of a higher education for the young men and women of our state and nation, and to that end provide a fund to be held in trust for the same, and to select a proper school or university where the same would continue in perpetuity, I will, devise and bequeath all of the real and personal property that I possess and of which I die seized to the Trustees of Indiana University, Bloomington, Indiana, to be held by them and their successors in office forever, the *Income* only to be used and applied in the support and maintenance of a *Chair* in *Philosophy* in said institution, and to be dedicated and forever known as "The Mahlon Powell Professorship in Philosophy" of said University.

In accordance with the provisions of this bequest, the Trustees of Indiana University have established a Chair in Philosophy on The Mahlon Powell Foundation. Each year a Visiting Professor will be invited to fill this Chair. The fourth lecturer on The Mahlon Powell Foundation is President Emeritus William Lowe Bryan of Indiana University.

HERMAN B WELLS
PRESIDENT, INDIANA UNIVERSITY

To My Most Sympathetic,
Keenly Discriminating,
and Austerely Truthful
Counselor

CHARLOTTE LOWE BRYAN

LES FAMILLES D'ESPRITS

Les familles véritables et *naturelles* des hommes ne sont pas si nombreuses ; quand on a un peu observé de ce côté et opéré sur des quantités suffisantes, on reconnait combien les natures diverses d'esprits, d'organisations, se rapportent à certains types, à certains chefs principaux. Tel contemporain notable qu'on a bien vu et compris, vous explique et vous pose toute une série de morts, du moment que la réelle ressemblance entre eux vous est manifeste et que certains caractères de famille ont saisi le regard. C'est absolument comme en botanique pour les plantes, en zoologie pour les espèces animales. Il y a l'histoire naturelle morale, la méthode (à peine ébauchée) des familles naturelles d'esprits. Un individu bien observé se rapporte vite à l'espèce qu'on n'a vue que de loin, et l'éclaire.

SAINTE-BEUVE, *Port-Royal,* I, 55.

CONTENTS

INTRODUCTION

I PROPOSE a study of some of the varied ways in which men try to learn what they wish to know. Consider, for example, the divergent ways employed by these five men: the hunter Daniel Boone, the scientist Galileo, the philosopher Hegel, the poet Keats, and St. John. There are likenesses in the methods of these men. I am interested now in their differences. Boone was not schooled in the methods of what the universities call philosophy or science. Neither Hegel nor Galileo would have recognized Boone as a colleague. However, Boone had ways of finding out what he especially wished to know. They were ways which had the merit of enabling him to survive in the Kentucky wilderness—a success which neither Hegel nor Galileo, nor Keats nor St. John could have achieved (barring miracle) by any knowledge or way of learning which they had. Each of the four, speaking from his own standpoint, could pass critical judgment on the method and knowledge of Boone. All of them would have been lost in Boone's Kentucky.

Galileo was interested, among other things, in the movements of the sun and the planets. He did not look for the knowledge which he desired to any such man as Boone, however keen in his own affairs, nor to Plato, nor to Aquinas, nor to any metaphysician, however profound, nor to poet, nor to saint. Galileo followed another way, a way more in use since than before his time, and by that way he arrived at conclusions concerning the solar system which have been recognized as of epoch-making importance.

George William Frederick Hegel was a philosopher. He sought for a rationalized view of all reality. Hegel's philosophy provides a place for everything—for Boone's wilderness and for Boone, for Galileo's planets, for Keats and all poetry and all arts, for St. John and for all religions, from primitive devil worship to the philosopher's intellectual apprehension of the divine Absolute. But none of these men would recognize himself in Hegel's picture of him.

Keats saw a Darien and a wilderness such as Boone, stout Cortez, and Balboa saw, and the ocean that lay beyond, but with other eyes than theirs—eyes that had no need of Galileo's telescope. Keats saw beauty, and also another facet of the same reality. He believed that the poet has a vision of truth which is denied all other men.

St. John aspired to see God. He believed that the pure in heart shall see God.

Each of these men is one of many who are like him in the kind of knowledge which they especially desire and in the way of arriving at such knowledge.

I call these groups families of minds.

I owe the phrase to Sainte-Beuve, who uses it

to distinguish groups of authors who differ profoundly in disposition and prevailing mood. Some have the temper of ironic Voltaire; others, the spirit of the devout Bossuet; others, the mathematical mind of Descartes. I use the expression to designate groups which differ one from another still more profoundly. The five human groups which I have named, and other such major and minor families of minds, present an important field of study. The easiest and the usual way of studying such groups of human beings is to adopt the point of view of one of them and to judge all the others from that standpoint. Examples of such one-point-of-view judgments of all other points of view are heard on every side and fill the literature of the world. There is another way, illustrated in part —only in part—by the best anthropologist in his studies of alien races. He belongs himself to one race, but he does not begin or even end with the view that the ways of his race are right and the ways of other races wrong. His first concern is to apprehend the ways of an alien race as viewed by its own folk. The enormous difficulty which a man of the white race has in understanding men of the black, yellow, or red races is realized only by those who have seriously undertaken the task. There are those who say that the task is impossible:

> East is East and West is West
> And never the twain shall meet.

Nevertheless, there are men who dare this task. They go perhaps for years to Central Africa. They think black. They live black. And so, after years, they approach an apprehension of the black as he understands himself. It is my view that the human groups represented by Boone, Galileo, Hegel, Keats, and St. John, to name no others, are, in the kinds of knowledge which they seek and in their ways of searching for that knowledge, almost or quite as far from one another as are the major races of mankind. Deep are the affinities between those who belong to the same family of minds, though born in different continents and in different millennia. Deep are the misunderstandings and hostilities between men of diverse families of minds though born under the same roof. It may seem in this case, also, that no one can understand any one of those groups except the one to which he belongs. A way is opened by those men, greater or less, who belong to more than one of those families of minds.

I discuss now only a small part of the whole program which I have suggested. I propose to consider certain of the historic wars between families of minds.

I should like to know better than I do why it is that men come to be so far apart as scientist and philosopher sometimes are, or as scientist and poet sometimes are. I suggest a reason.

To begin with, men differ in what they want

most—in what they are hungry for. Some kind of hunger is at the root of everything in life. What a man wants most he attends to most. Attention has two inevitable effects. What a man attends to he sees better. What he does not attend to he sees less well or not at all. At every moment seeing clearly one image on the retina makes one oblivious of other images on the retina. And after seeing clearly day after day what we most want to see, we do not see and finally cannot see what we have ignored. There is the story of Charles Darwin. He lamented that, after a lifetime of absorption in science, his youthful interest in art had died. His expression is that a part of his brain had become atrophied. Consider in contrast the case of Dean Swift. He was a university man. He had what is called a liberal education; that is, he was master of classical learning. He was of a genius only below the very greatest. But in a time when science was rising to greatness about him, in the very year of the death of one of the greatest scientists who had ever lived, Swift poured out upon science and scientists the devastating lava of his scorn.

Whoever follows one vocation intensively and exclusively grows blind to all the world outside —becomes atrophied, as Darwin says, and may become intolerant and savage like Swift. This I conceive to be at least part of the reason for what I have called wars of families of minds.

However, there are men who by reason of native disposition and by following diverse occupations come to belong profoundly to more than one family of minds. There is Aristotle, scientist and metaphysician. There is Leonardo, scientist, engineer, artist. There is Goethe, dramatist, lyric poet, scientist, man of affairs. There are many others, the greater and the lesser. Such men provide the best and perhaps the only real bridge between human groups which are far apart and often hostile each to the other.

I shall consider these misunderstandings and hostilities[1] in three chapters as follows:

I. The Scholar and the Unschooled Man
II. Scholar against Scholar
III. Scholar and Poet

1. In the latter part of each chapter, the author states his own view upon the controversial questions considered. Consideration of the Seer under III is deferred.

WARS OF FAMILIES OF MINDS

I

THE SCHOLAR AND THE UNSCHOOLED MAN

THE unschooled man had a long first inning in historic and prehistoric time. He has had one great undeniable success. He has survived. When other animal species stronger and swifter than he have perished, our unacademic ancestor met all the dangers and defeated or escaped them. The scholar who regards with contempt the ideas and achievements of the unschooled multitude must admit that, by their rules of thumb, they have survived to give him his chance on this planet. The undeniable success of men devoid of science, the astonishing ingenuities of Eskimos and Africans out of all contact with civilization, the achievements of common men in prehistoric and in historic time account for the confidence of the nonscientific man in his methods and account in part for his suspicion and distrust of the methods and results of a scholarship which lies outside his experience. Moreover, the distrust and hostility of the unschooled man for the scholar have been encouraged and strengthened by men from other families of minds. I shall cite several notable instances which show the reality and intensity of the war against the scholar by the man in the street, often encouraged by the artist.

Aristophanes and the Athenian People against Socrates

I recall first the rising anger of the Athenian people against the scholars of the fifth century—an anger which culminated in the death of Socrates and which later threatened the life of Aristotle. According to Plato, they were incited to it by Aristophanes, the comic poet. The master of comedy embodied his foe dramatically in the master of philosophy, Socrates. He exhibited a stage Socrates swinging in a hammock among *The Clouds*, devising ways of teaching youth how to escape their debts and how to make the worse appear the better reason. The highly sophisticated Athenian multitude must have shouted with delight to recognize on the stage the grotesque figure of Socrates, whom they saw in person on the street every day. The appeal of Aristophanes to the man in the street against the philosopher is what George Cohan knows as sure-fire comedy. It is certain of winning bursts of laughter. It arouses also hostility. The man in the street resents the scholar's pretension to superior wisdom and is disposed to strike back. The Athenians struck back. Galton attributes to the Athenians of the fifth century B.C. a level of intelligence decidedly higher than that of the English of the nineteenth century A.D., but the Athenian people could not comprehend and finally would not tolerate the scholars who had made part of the glory of their city. They put to death their Divine Gadfly. Here is a typical battle between families of minds—on the one side the scholar, on the other the man in the street, reinforced by the comic poet.

Molière Incites Paris against the Scholars

Look now at Molière. Nothing is more characteristic of this supreme master of high comedy and low than his appeal to a modern Athens, that is, Paris, against the scholar and his learning. France in the seventeenth century, like Greece twenty-two centuries earlier, had of course its futile pretenders to learning, but also scholars in philosophy and in science whom the universities still hold in honor. One needs only recall Gassendi, Paré,

Descartes, Pascal. Molière knew, or knew of, those learned men. He had a college education. He was introduced to Aristotle. He seems to have come under the influence of Gassendi, who professed the atomic philosophy of Lucretius. There is some evidence that Molière translated at least part of the *De Rerum Natura* of Lucretius. Whatever he knew of the learning of his time, the master of comedy as writer and as actor again and again enticed Paris to laughter against the scholar. The farce comedy, *Les Précieuses ridicules*, is directed against women of the lower middle class who ape the sophisticated words and ways which cultivated women of the aristocracy have made fashionable. *Les Femmes savantes* is high comedy directed against women of the upper middle class. The ladies have a club. At the club they have a matinee-idol poet and gather about him in adoration of his inanities. They revel in what they take to be art, philosophy, culture, and they unite in scorn of the ignoble vocation of wife and mother. It is said that Madame de Rambouillet, founder of the first salon in which nobles, poets, scholars, and cultivated women met for high discourse, saw with admiration the caricature of her salon in *Les Précieuses ridicules*. It may be that the incomparable Madame de Sévigné viewed with like tolerance and amusement the caricature of learned women by the incomparable Molière. Molière was serious in his attack upon learning in women. He quotes somewhere with approval the saying of a nobleman of an earlier time that a woman needs to know nothing except the difference between her husband's shirt and his jacket.

In five plays, ranging from slapstick farce to high comedy, Molière attacks the physician. His attack reached its climax in the great *Malade imaginaire*. Through the shrewd, unschooled housemaid (who is often his spokesman in other plays), he pours ridicule upon the absurd pretensions of the doctors who prey upon her employer. The invalid's brother-in-law presents what was certainly Molière's own considered belief, that the hidden springs of our natures are mysteries of which the doctors know nothing, covering up their ignorance and bewildering their victims with a babel of learned words.

In the farce comedy, *Le Mariage forcé*, Molière attacks the philosophers. He shows one of them in a furious quarrel over logic-chopping words. The other is a philosophic skeptic who will admit nothing whatever as certainly true until he is made certain that the exasperated Sganarelle is beating him with a stick. In the mighty tragi-comedy, *Don Juan,* Molière pours scorn upon the attempt to defend religious faith by evidence from the sciences. He does this with dramatic effectiveness by putting a farrago of such arguments in the mouth of the clown Sganarelle. The serious *Critique de l'École des Femmes* exhibits the divergence and conflict between the scholar and the artist, between the laws of comedy as viewed by Aristotle and the laws of comedy as viewed by the master comedian. Here meet in battle two great families of minds—the family of Aristotle and the family of Molière.

Dean Swift and John Bull against the Scientists

Look now at Dean Swift, another literary genius who invited his public to ridicule and hostility against the scholar. Swift lived in an age when modern science was reaching its stride. The universities engrave upon their walls the names of those who made those years illustrious in mathematics, astronomy, physics, chemistry, and physiology. That era began with the Copernican theory of the solar system and reached its climax in Newton's law of gravitation.

Swift was not wholly ignorant of these

achievements. He was a university man. He had what is called a liberal education, but his liberalism did not include understanding or tolerance of science. In the year of Newton's death, 1727, Swift published *Gulliver's Travels.* "As every schoolboy knows" (since every schoolboy is supposed to have had *Gulliver* in his Christmas stocking), he poured out a torrent of ridicule upon the science of his time. In simple words which betrayed an underlying volcano of passion he incited unscientific John Bull to join in savage laughter. Scientists are pictured as living upon an island which floats among the clouds. Members of the Academy of Lagado (which stands for the British Royal Society) are found engaged in every sort of fantastic scientific folly. They are extracting sunbeams from cucumbers, which, said Gulliver, would soon supply the governor's garden with sunshine all year round at reasonable rates. They are powdering ice into gunpowder. Blind men are mixing colors for painters by taste and smell. Marble is being softened for pillows. There is a machine which enables the most ignorant person to write at a reasonable charge books on poetry, philosophy, or what you please. No one answers when you speak to him. You must recall the professor from his world of futile scientific dreams by a blow on the head with a bladder.

English science was not killed by the scorn of Swift but went prosperously on its way. But unscientific John Bull almost down to our time shared Swift's contempt for the scholar. Distrust of the expert—there you have the typical Englishman, and one must add the typical American, through the centuries of modern science down to the World War. "The damned college professor"—Poultney Bigelow says that was the characteristic word of John Bull for the scholar. Lord Haldane, speaking in the British Parliament before the World War, said that there were more chemists in one German plant than in all the factories in England. He warned the Empire that, however successful in the past, British rules of thumb could not finally win in war or in peace against German science. It took the World War to convert John Bull from Swift's scorn of the damned college professor.

American Distrust of the Expert

It took the same overwhelming experience to make the American businessman, manufacturer, and man of affairs realize that common sense minus science cannot compete in war or in peace with common sense plus science. Some Americans are not yet converted. I cite a few illustrations of the deep-seated American distrust of the scholar. In 1862 provision was made by Congress for a College of Agriculture in each of our states. For at least fifty years the hardest task of those colleges was not to discover what should be done upon the farms but to make the farmers believe that the science of agriculture had anything of value for them. What is this nonsense about the chemistry of soils?—send us a man who works in dirt. Let me recall two cases which fell under my observation. Some time before the World War, I rode for several hours in company with a member of Congress from eastern Massachusetts, graduate of Harvard, son-in-law of a United States Senator. As we rode through the rich farms of northern Indiana, I spoke of the excellent services of Purdue University to our farmers. Said the Congressman in substance: "I do not believe in the schools of agriculture nor in the United States Department of Agriculture. They give me nothing but useless theories. When I want advice for my Virginia farm, I depend upon my neighbor farmers." If the Harvard Brahman scorns the agricultural scientist, why should more be expected of the farmer in the Middle West?

There was the same resistance from the hardheaded businessmen against the counsels of the scientific engineer. A prosperous Chicago manufacturer has written a volume in which he attacks the schools of engineering as vehemently as Swift attacked the scientists of his floating island. He renounced the lore of the scientific engineers. He would have no college graduate in his factories. He had found his way to success and would find the rest of the way by nothing but old-fashioned horse sense.

For twenty years the battle against the scientist was fought here in this university town. The city had a water problem. Water had been found in one area, but the city grew faster than the water supply. There were water famines one after another, each worse than the last. A group of university scientists and two groups of professional engineers reported after thorough investigation that the old area could never provide enough water for the growing city but that another near-by area could supply water for a city several times as large as this one. Battle was joined between the horse-sense man and the scientist.

The battle went on and on, the famines grew worse and worse, until at last a group of citizens ended the famine and the war by going for water where the scientific engineers told them to go.

From Ignorant Hostility to Ignorant Subservience

Today the torrent of scientific inventions whose success all can see is having its effect upon the attitude of the man on the farm and the man in the factory toward science. More and more of them see the new light and accept its guidance. But this has led also to another strange, socially important result. Many of the multitude have been converted from ignorant hostility to ignorant subservience toward whatever calls itself science. Frauds of every sort have been quick to take advantage of this new kind of popular credulity. A public which once bought cure-alls said to have been discovered by an Indian medicine doctor now buys cure-alls said to have been discovered by a professor in the University of Vienna or psychological recipes for transforming a weak, wabbling failure into a victorious master of men.

A study of advertisements through each decade of the last century would exhibit this progressive conversion of the unschooled population from ignorant hostility to ignorant subservience toward what they understand to be science.

The Scholar Is Not Always Right

There is another side to the story of the scholar and those who distrust his results. The scholar is not always right. He is never wholly and certainly right. He tries to isolate a bit of the universe and find out the truth about that bit. But no bit of the universe can ever be isolated. He measures with precision, but the very devices he employs to secure precision may exclude essential factors, and those factors may presently rise up and bring his work to nought. He tries if possible to treat his findings mathematically so as to bring all of them into consistent unity, but a mathematical formula is sometimes a trap within which one grows blind to facts that do not fit the formula. Always the vast unknown lies outside the laboratory door ready to break in and upset one's most confident conclusion.

So it can happen—so it does happen—in the war between science and the rules of thumb that the confident scientist is wrong and the wilderness hunter or the dirt farmer right. This fact I shall take occasion later to consider more at length.

The War between the Scientist and the Unschooled Man Goes On

The war between science and rule of thumb is not over. In many a school board, town council, and legislature the scientist is still the scorned and damned college professor. This war approaches an end as science and common sense unite where material things are concerned. But it is still far otherwise where human affairs are concerned, as in economics, politics, sociology, psychology, education. The scholars in these fields share the faith that the way of enlightenment is not by rule of thumb but by exact, verified, organized knowledge. They have enlisted first a few, then hundreds, then thousands of competent men in all civilized lands. They find place in all universities. They have produced great literatures. They are now more than ever before called into council by industry and government. Nevertheless, the scientists who deal with human affairs are far from such victory as has come to the engineers. For one thing, there are scholars in other fields, on the one hand physicists, on the other hand classicists, who vigorously, sometimes vehemently, deny the right of the so-called social scientists to be recognized as scientists at all. For another, the behavior of a population is more complicated and unpredictable than the behavior of known chemicals in a glass tube.

So the horse-sense man who now trusts the scientist's recipe for soap may still scorn the counsel of economist, sociologist, and psychologist. It is sufficient to cite the present war for and against the college professors whom the President of the United States calls to his council table. I shall at present leave those engaged in that battle to fight it out among themselves, in order to speak more at length on that one of the sciences of human nature with which I have had most acquaintance—a science in which I am Rip Van Winkle—psychology.

The Rise of Modern Psychology

The human mind has been studied in all the ways that anything has been studied. All the families of minds try to understand human nature. There is Abraham Lincoln's way. There is the way of poet and seer, of Shakespeare and Dante. There is the way of the philosopher, of Plato and Hegel. Then rose the way of science. Inevitably men of science came to say: The methods of exact science win more and more success in dealing with things; let us now apply those methods to the study of human nature. Let us disentangle the study of mind from metaphysics and make psychology a true science side by side with physics. No doubt this idea lay long in germ undeveloped. About three quarters of a century ago the germ began a vigorous growth, especially in Germany. The German beginners were men of unexcelled fitness to do what they undertook—Johannes Müller, Weber, Fechner, Wundt, Helmholtz—men eminent in mathematics, chemistry, physics, physiology, and also well learned in philosophy. They turned the methods of which they were masters upon the problems of the human mind and human behavior. As physicists they sought to establish psychophysics. As physiologists they sought to establish physiological psychology. Scientists in other countries—France, England, Italy, America—by the same methods and by different methods sought the same goal, the establishment of a science of psychology as an integral part of the whole body of science recognized by the universities.

One result at any rate is manifest. There is now an army of professional psychologists.

They are in the universities, colleges, teacher-training schools, even in many high schools, and they are outside the schools in many types of industry. And because there is a living for so many psychologists, a throng of young people are coming up through the schools to make psychology their profession.

And now, what is the actual outcome of these seventy-five years of enormous endeavor to create a science of psychology? Ask the psychologists. Ask three questions:

1. Are there as the outcome of the studies in psychology definite results which all of you or most of you recognize as valid and valuable?

The psychologists will answer almost or quite unanimously in the affirmative. If you then ask for details, they can give you a list so great and so varied that no one psychologist professes to have adequate knowledge of all of them. In this respect psychology resembles chemistry, for example, which has so many specialties that no one chemist can be master of all of them.

2. Is there somewhere a statement of the fundamental principles of the science of psychology which all psychologists or most of them accept as satisfactory?

The answers are not unanimous.

In his recent, all-too-brief autobiography, Professor Woodworth writes: "Outsiders sitting in our meetings sometimes get the impression of mutual hostility within our group, but I am sure that this is a false impression. My own impression is one of fundamental solidarity, along with the freedom of discussion that comes from direct handling of the subject matter." This weighty judgment has support from many other psychologists as, for example, Professor Joseph Jastrow.

There is, however, an opposed view. In the Clark University volume entitled *Psychologies of 1930*, twenty-four psychologists present what one of them, Professor Spearman, denominates "ten warring schools of Psychology." Professor Heidbreder's *Seven Psychologies* begins as follows:

> It is something of a paradox that systems of psychology flourish as they do on American soil. Psychology, especially in the United States, has risked everything on being science; and science on principle refrains from speculation that is not permeated and stabilized by fact. Yet there is not enough fact in the whole science of psychology to make a single solid system.

These critical statements do not represent skepticism of psychology. They represent what the writers believe to be its present status. Professor Heidbreder writes further:

> They [systems of psychology] can best be understood not as statements of scientific fact, not as summaries of existing knowledge, but as ways and means of arriving at knowledge, as temporary but necessary stages in the development of a science, as creations of workers who, in a confusing and sometimes depressing enterprise, must keep not only their poise but also their verve.

A test of the present situation in psychology may be made by attempting to find a textbook which psychologists generally will consent to use with beginning classes. It so happens that as a member of the State Board of Education of Indiana it has been my duty each five years to vote for high-school textbooks in chemistry, physics, botany, zoölogy. I have turned, of course, for advice to scientists in those fields. Equally, of course, the men rate the books variously, according to their individual preferences. But always there have been plenty of elementary texts which all regarded as acceptable introductions to those sciences. I have quite failed to find any such generally acceptable textbook in the elements of psychology. I have been assured that there is no such book. I have heard a widely used book written by a psychologist who shares the view of Professor Woodworth characterized by a vigorous young psychologist as a menace to psychology.

I have heard Professor Woodworth's view defended in this way: Men who seem farthest apart, as for example the late Professor McDougall and the most extreme behaviorists, use different language, but, as a rule, mean the same things. It is my impression that this is true when the two men discuss matters of observed fact, but not at all true when they discuss underlying theory. The differences in underlying theory are fundamental with both men and come out in what they write and in what they teach.

I do not refer to emotional hostilities, such as the assault of Titchener upon James or Münsterberg's return attack upon Titchener. Psychologists sometimes fight, but not more than men in any other science. As a rule, they are personally cordial to one another. The differences that divide them are fundamental ones of conviction as to underlying theory, as deep as any differences of beliefs that divide men. The creeds of Moslems and Christians at the time of the Crusades were not further apart than are the theories of present-day psychologists. Moslem and Christian agreed in the belief in God and in the reality and immortality of souls, while in our day there are psychologists of high standing who base their psychologies upon the belief in the reality of the soul and others who do not believe in the existence of souls anywhere in the universe.

Do these unreconciled differences dampen the zeal of the psychologists? Not at all. Rather quite the contrary. When religious sects fight, the zeal of each for its faith flames highest. So now the psychologist who has found the only true way presses forward in the confidence that other psychologists will finally see the light as he sees it and be saved from psychological damnation. In spite of all differences, there is, I daresay, no other group of scientists more confident of the future of their science than are the psychologists. Extremists and moderates alike rely upon two undeniable facts. The one is the body of particular achievements which all recognize as valid. The other is the body of men and women, perhaps not excelled in any other science, who in full faith and with unflagging zeal devote themselves to the discovery of a science of psychology. Personally, I share their faith, though at the same time I believe that wilderness man and poet and seer have knowledge of human reality which so far lies beyond the reach of scientific psychology.

I wish to note one unfortunate consequence of the division of psychology into sects. While the individual who becomes a psychologist finds his way at last to his psychological faith after contact with many teachers and books, the individual who takes only an elementary course in psychology acquires some one of the contending psychologies by the accident which brings him to that class.

3. To what extent is present-day scientific psychology able to direct successfully the conduct of human affairs in matters of major policy?

Applied psychology seems now generally victorious. It is becoming more and more popular with the man in the street, who used to be hostile to science but has been partially converted by the torrent of scientific inventions that he can see, and has become more and more docile to anything that calls itself science. He is, therefore, often willing to pay extravagantly for the promises and prophecies of anyone who calls himself a psychologist. Responsible psychologists try to protect the public from the fakers and also from those among their own number who make overenthusiastic claims for their professional advice.

Meanwhile, responsible psychologists of the highest standing meet the more and more frequent calls of individuals, schools, corporations, and governments for advice based upon the findings of scientific psychology. In a word, applied psychology has become a profession, or rather a group of professions, which claims a place by the side of the profession of medicine.

However, my question now is: How does applied psychology compare for example with engineering in dealing with major problems of policy? When there is a question of making an interoceanic canal, technical science, through a group of diverse associated experts, brings to the door of the government reliable counsel not only as to the best mixture of concrete and a thousand other such details, but also as to where to make the canal and whether it is practicable to undertake it at all. Like all experts these technicians may go wrong, as De Lesseps did at Panama. But also they often go right, as Goethals and Gorgas did at Panama, when they and associated experts found the way which civilized man had been looking for since the time of Columbus.

But now, when it is not a matter of geology

or yellow fever but a correspondingly great matter of human behavior, how successfully can scientific psychology advise what to do?

Some years ago I put this question to six psychologists who have become university presidents. Later, I wrote to a seventh, and also to several other psychologists who are not university presidents.

My question was:

To what extent has scientific psychology provided you with definite guidance in your administrative activities?

Scientific astronomy tells the astronomer that he may see an eclipse in Maine on the 31st of August and in exactly what direction his telescope must be pointed in order to photograph the eclipse. Does scientific psychology provide you with anything remotely corresponding to that in dealing with the behavior of those whose behavior you must deal with?

There are some useful intelligence tests and some helpful suggestions with regard to learning. But in dealing with the groups which concern you, with the students, parents, alumni, the public—in what ways has scientific psychology come to your substantial aid? An engineer of 1932 has enormous advantage over an engineer of 1861–65 because of the advance in the sciences which guide him. In what way or degree does the advance in scientific psychology since the death of Abraham Lincoln give you advantage over Lincoln in dealing with human affairs?

The following are letters or extracts from letters which the authors have graciously permitted me to quote:

From President James R. Angell, Yale University, July 23, 1932.

I SHOULD say that in my strictly administrative work as an executive I have never availed myself of formal psychological technique. The issues which have commonly come directly to me for handling have rarely been of a kind to permit this—and when they have, other considerations have made their employment impracticable or inexpedient. On the other hand, in dealing with people, and especially in framing judgments about them, my impression is that my psychological training has bred in me attitudes—and perhaps prejudices—that have played a rather important part in my decisions.

And more recently, in July, 1939, President Angell writes:

If I were employing certain types of men in any number today, I think I should avail myself of certain of the test procedures. But for the special problems I am now facing these are not relevant.

From President Leonard Carmichael, Tufts College, July 3, 1939.

When the question arose as to whether or not I should accept the Presidency of Tufts College from which I had graduated some eighteen years previously, I debated the matter for a long time. I was extremely happy as a teacher and an investigator in the field of psychology. To me, however, psychology is the science of human behavior. All that I had done in my work in psychology had been indirectly aimed at a further understanding of the laws which govern the activities of human beings. Should I accept an administrative position in which I would have an opportunity to deal with a number of human problems as a psychologist or should I not? Two answers to this question suggested themselves: (1) Psychology is still in its infancy. Nothing that I know is sufficiently advanced to make application to the real problems of the actual world possible. Therefore, I should continue during my life span in scientific psychological work with the hope that ultimately, as the generations pass, a sufficient body of knowledge will be assembled to make practical engineering applications of psychology possible. (2) In spite of its obvious incompleteness, psychology already provides sufficient rules and insight into the basis of human conduct to make the administration of an educational institution a task in applied psychology. To shirk this opportunity when it offers would be to turn aside from a chance to put into action the principles that I have been studying and teaching.

So, after long consideration, I decided to adopt the course of action indicated in the second of the alternatives just discussed.

Now, at the conclusion of my first year as a college president, what is my decision? Was I correct or not in my choice? Possibly because I am by temperament optimistic, I can only say that it seems to me that my choice was a wise one and that I feel that an understanding of psychology is especially useful to me in my present position. No two human beings are alike, and yet there are many motives and attitudes shared in common by most adult civilized Americans. The memory of this fact, together with the recognition of the important part played by custom and tradition in the lives of men, has helped me to realize that changes in a social organism, such as a college, should come about as a result of evolution rather than as a result of "special creation."

It may be—to summarize what I have said above—that those aspects of psychology which are most important for the administrator are similar to those aspects of psychology which are important for the psychiatrist. I cannot help feeling, however, that the one who approaches college administration from a psychological, psychiatric and biological point of view has a great advantage over one who comes to this work of administration from a life of scholarship in the physical sciences, the so-called humanities or certain fields in the social sciences.

From President H. W. Chase, University of Illinois, July 20, 1932.

I HAVE often speculated on the point you raise in your letter of July 18th about the practical value of the training in psychology that I once had. I think it is a very interesting question. I believe there is something in it.

I think from the particular brand of psychology that Stanley Hall taught us that I got an attitude toward young people and their problems that has been helpful administratively. I think perhaps I should say that fundamentally I got an attitude toward education that has always stayed with me from my teaching days, namely, that what was going on in education was not merely a matter to be argued in terms of opinion and tradition but that it was possible to take a more objective attitude toward its processes and products. In short, it seems to me that my general attitude and outlook were pretty well colored by the psychological background. So far as dealing with particular problems in which human relationships are concerned, I mean with individual faculty cases or questions of public opinion, I would be less confident of any extent of psychological training. I don't see much result there. It seems to me that my methods have been largely empirical. I know I look back on some of my early attempts with a good deal of amusement and the interesting thing to me is that after thirteen years of this administrative game it seems to me that every problem of that kind is about as perplexing as ever and that my percentage of mistakes in practical psychology is high, though I don't believe it is as high as it was thirteen years ago. I think, however, that sad experience and not psychology has been responsible for whatever upward trend that particular administrative curve may have shown.

In short, it seems to me that I did at least get two things: First, a permanent interest in young people's problems, and second, the idea that education as a process is a thing we ought to try to look at objectively and to study and measure and experiment with, rather than to take for granted. I am afraid that is pretty vague. It may be that other former psychologists would be able to see much more in detail the effects of their training than I can and mine may be much more effectual than I can indicate. I should be very much interested to know what some of the other men say.

And on June 24, 1939, President Chase writes:

I don't know that I have changed my mind in any respect since I wrote that letter.

From President L. D. Coffman, University of Minnesota, July 27, 1939.

The question, "To what extent has scientific psychology provided you with definite guidance in your administrative activities?" is not easy to answer. It has not provided me with patterns of experience that I can apply to situations with the same certainty that an astronomer can direct his telescope nor with the same certainty that a physician can diagnose a disease, and yet scientific psychology has developed a type of mind closely akin to that of the astronomer or that of the physician. . . .

If I were to name any one contribution which scientific psychology has made to me I should say that the most significant of them all is the desire to know what the facts are in disposing of any particular case or situation. . . .

Again, when we found that the representatives of the various scientific departments of the University differed enormously in their views as to the methods that should be employed in the teaching of science, some said that elementary science should be taught one hour a day every day of the week; others said, two hours a day; some said, every other day; some said, by having a demonstration before the class by the instructors; others, by having the old fashioned question and answer recitations; others, by making use of the laboratory; and still others, by turning the students loose in the laboratory with a manual. My position was, why should not the University find out what is the best way. . . .

And so I might continue with dozens of illustrations. Each one has led to a study with the result that the University has developed an experimental attitude toward education. . . .

From Professor Richard M. Elliott, Department of Psychology, University of Minnesota, January 3, 1940.

PSYCHOLOGY has, I believe, been an aid and advantage to me in administrative dealings with people for reasons which include the following:

1. Training in science is training in skepticism. To every scientific generalization there is appended an implicit footnote "this may someday be proved wrong, or inexact." In every experiment, one always remembers, there *may* lurk an uncontrolled variable. So a person who has thoroughly absorbed the scientific temper ought to be more than usually aware at every move in life: "I may be wrong. Perhaps I have overlooked the most essential factor." This makes for a general attitude of caution and deliberation in whatever one undertakes to do. Note that even Thorndike has not attempted to disprove transfer of general *attitudes*.

2. Psychology often deals with intangibles

requiring the closest attention to the distinction between what is observed or physically manipulated and what is inferred. Psychology, for this reason, has been forced to be extremely sophisticated about its methods. The research done by medical men, to take an example, often seems crude to the psychologist because the former, relying on test-tubes, balances, and other physical instruments, believes that he has his stuff right in his grip, and that an experiment with physical materials has a certain indisputable character which needs no refined analysis. But the psychologist cannot often be so sure of himself. Certainly he has given more thought to "significant differences," probable errors, and other statistical refinements.

This point may seem at first sight to be without bearing on administrative techniques but I think a case might be made out to the contrary, again along the line of the transfer of general attitudes.

3. Modern psychology has exorcised the ghosts, free-willish imps, "good" angels and "bad" devils, which the man on the street too often sees as the instigators of human actions. Mental activity, psychology holds, is a highly specialized form of protoplasmic activity. Whatever happens has its natural and inevi-

table conditions. If you want to change a result then you must change the conditions which have brought it about and will do so again unless you alter them. It is a waste of breath merely to denounce what you do not like, and the more emotion you put into doing so the worse showing you make. Go to work influencing human nature as you do physical nature. Try to become an engineer, i.e. one who can control in proportion as he understands.

I fancy that I can explain many of the predicaments which I watch people slip into, and trace to its source much of the friction between personalities which is an ever-present cause of human unhappiness, in their failure to grasp this fundamental position.

From Dean George Ferguson, Jr., University of Virginia, July 12, 1939.

I AM not at all certain that it is proper to judge psychology in the way you indicate, but I am also not at all certain that such knowledge of psychology as I may have has aided me in the administration of this office.

From President W. A. Jessup, The State University of Iowa, August 25, 1932.

I HAVE been intrigued by your question of

July 18th. I wish I could give you a better answer as I think the question is of immense importance.

I do not believe that psychology has meant to me at all what mathematics has meant to the astronomer. . . .

It seems to me that psychologists have made an excellent beginning and many isolated bits of information have been accumulated but we have lacked the integrated minds needed in the matter of tying together the information we now have so that it may become meaningful for practical situations on a large scale.

My impression of the research which has been carried forward in great commercial enterprises has been in the direction of finding needs for information and then projecting an infinite series of inquiries all along the line. These inquiries have then been integrated by somebody or by a directing group in an attempt to get an answer to a series of definite questions.

The fact that the pure scientist, including the psychologist, works in isolation contributes enormously to the number of separate units of knowledge. A master mind might well direct the isolated scientist to study neglected fields until the gaps are filled.

Thus you see my conclusion is that we lack an Aristotle or a Plato. . . .

From Chancellor E. H. Lindley, The University of Kansas, October 3, 1939.

THE high hopes of twenty-five years ago have decidedly not been fully realized. The level has, however, been raised as the bed of the Mississippi by the steady deposit of silt from the highlands. We are still far from the complete directive psychology.

Gains have been made in—

1. The field of mental measurements (intelligence, achievement, aptitude and attitude, and vocational tests).

2. Abnormal psychology. The psychiatric approach has been fruitful. In spite of the excesses of the Freudians we are in possession of better analyses of personality and motivation.

3. Some advance in our knowledge of the learning process.

Some of the younger men report a convergence of warring sects. That is hopeful.

From Dean William F. Russell, Teachers College, Columbia University, July 11, 1939.

IT is difficult for me to be specific about the

services that psychology has rendered to me. I feel quite sure that what I learned from Thorndike has been almost invaluable, particularly my understanding of how people learn, the studies of mental fatigue, and the use of the instinctive equipment of man.

I have had to deal with several cases of severe mental illness that have caused me great administrative trouble. In these cases I have been much helped by psychologists and psychiatrists. In fact, in one severe case, these scholars were able to chart for me the exact times when the case would enter into a period of depression, when I might expect trouble.

From President Walter Dill Scott, Northwestern University, July 21, 1932.

I BELIEVE that my study of psychology has benefited me, but it has done so indirectly rather than directly. It has given me a point of view that has caused me to realize the existence of personal differences, and has made the procedure of handling men a real problem and one that is fundamentally interesting as well as valuable.

My study of social psychology, and particularly the applications of social psychology, have, I believe, been of value to me in my administrative position. Even though we do not know as much as we should about the motives for human action, the consideration of such motives is of importance in preparing material which is planned to secure action. . . . In attempting to influence one business man I presented the project as a great bargain. He invested several million dollars in the project and when he had signed the paper he stood up and said: "That's the best bargain I ever made." I had never used the word "bargain," but the whole attempt was to present the matter in that light. This illustration indicates what I have in mind. If I had not studied psychology I should never have analyzed motives in the way I now do.

June 24, 1939, President Scott wrote:

. . . It seems to me that my letter of July 21, 1932, expressed the facts. Since the date of my letter in all the world there have been only four gifts in excess of $5,000,000. Two of these have come to Northwestern. In the case of each of these gifts coming to Northwestern we carried on an extensive campaign in which we attempted to utilize all the psychology we had ever heard of. The fact that we were successful in these two campaigns of course does not indicate that the application of psychology was the dominant factor. I honestly believe it did help. . . .

Again I repeat, the fact that they worked is not conclusive evidence of anything.

From Dean H. L. Smith, School of Education, Indiana University, June 24, 1939.

GENERALLY speaking, I have not found my training in Psychology advantageous in determining major educational policies.

There is one exception, however, to this general statement. I have applied my knowledge of Educational Psychology in determining general policies that I have faced as a school administrator in determining the proper curriculum and methods of instruction and organization and administration that best fit the individual differences of pupils.

From Dr. George D. Stoddard, Dean of Graduate School, The State University of Iowa, January 4, 1940.

THE major contribution has come from social and abnormal psychology, perhaps from the great area which, for want of a better term, may be called mental hygiene. As we get at the needs, frustrations, anxieties, attitudes and aspirations of persons we deal with, there are opened up immense possibilities for the first-hand application of new insights and principles. Fortunately too there is a sufficient generality to these principles to enable us to follow certain lines of social contact known to be valuable in adjustment. For example, every person has areas of insecurity; every person is in need of some social and personal nourishment. I should say that frequently a knowledge of the particular problems of students and staff members is not so crucial as the general category into which their behavior has fallen. Thus at times a teacher or administrator is in a position to help students, one might say *en masse*, by paying close attention to their genuine needs for social enrichment.

From Professor Howard R. Taylor, University of Oregon, July, 1939.

I do not think the analogy between the application of our knowledge of natural science to engineering problems and our knowledge of psychology to problems of human engineering is really very close.

Psychology has learned how to use scientific methods in discovering truth in essentially the same way that physical scientists do, and eventually I believe the truth of the generalizations arrived at will be demonstrated by the pragmatic test of prediction. However, at present quantitative results in psychology enable us to judge the direction or trend in behavior which may reasonably be expected rather than to estimate with certainty the exact amount of it.

I should say modern psychology of the last twenty-five or thirty years is as useful to the administrators who are aware of it as the crude knowledge of materials or the interaction of practically unknown physical forces, for example, electricity, was to the engineer of sixty or seventy years ago.

In the first place, numerous studies have made us aware of the impossibility of accurately judging human personality and character by means of personal appearance or other external criteria, even by personal interview. Secondly, most of us, when we stop to think of it, are less inclined to overestimate the importance of conscious and rational factors in the initiation and control of human actions. Third, we have learned pretty well not to think of will, memory, intellect, or any other deification of psychological processes as faculties to be developed by practice or as independent forces to be counted on in estimating future behavior. In short, we are learning not to think of men as abstract entities but as organisms in dynamic relationship to all sorts of concrete environmental factors.

On the positive side, we have learned to make suitable allowances, both charitable and judgmental, for personal prejudice and similar bias in our own thinking and acting as well as in that of others. In any relatively unexplored field we have learned to put a good deal of trust in a consensus of expert opinion. Educationally now, we know how unreasonable it was to expect equivalent achievement from all students without regard to hereditary limitations, and at the same time we know that the proper stimulation of growth and learning in many important functions can add materially to individual proficiency. In recent years we have been taught to beware of the errors of atomism and too detailed analysis as a basis for understanding the functional wholes with which we are actually concerned. This is an idea which strikes directly at the root of most of our national and international problems today.

Psychology, of course, cannot tell us much about what would be required for a proper balance in the various aspects of our social life, but it provides overwhelming evidence of the supreme importance of functional harmony in both individual and social affairs.

My question was not a questionnaire. Each letter carries its own weighty judgment. I shall, however, give my own view, chiefly by extracts from the address which I gave as president of the American Psychological Association in 1903.

Theory and Practice[1]

Two of my predecessors have discussed from this chair the application of psychological theory to practice. Upon the principal question considered by them, as you know, they did not agree. However, difference of opinion upon this point is less surprising than unanimity would be. For time out of mind there have been not simply many divergent opinions as to the relations of theory and practice, but several types of such opinions persisting side by side century after century in collision. In one case it is believed that there is a philosophy which gives a finally valid account of all reality and which lays down the law for action in every field. In another case, it is not philosophy, but empirical science which, as it develops, is to free us from all the rules of thumb by which our ancestors groped and fumbled their way, and which is to show

1. President's address, American Psychological Association, St. Louis Meeting, December, 1903. *Psychological Review,* XI, 71 ff.

us with certainty and on rational grounds exactly what to do in every field. In a third case, it is not philosophy and not science, not systematic learning of any sort, but intuition, tact, common sense, which alone enable us to achieve success in any field.

The mention of these typical opinions brings to mind at once many great names which could be cited for and against each of them. I have sometimes tried to make the historic conflict of opinion upon this subject concrete for myself by imagining a committee selected from the great philosophers, scientists, poets, and men of affairs of history, the committee being directed, let us say, to act together as trustees of a village school. Plato, Cervantes, Comte, Prince Bismarck, Thomas Carlyle—whom you please—it would be easy to make up an interesting committee. The debates of that committee, the hopeless reciprocal misunderstandings, the scorn or compassion of each man for all the others, it would take Shakespeare to imagine. And the scene would be worthy of Shakespeare for, in a way, the most fundamental conflicts of the history of culture with all their humor and with all their gravity would be there. But even Shakespeare, I fear, could not imagine what the committee would decide to do. And yet decision as to what to do is the unavoidable task of most of us who profess psychology or indeed any science. For we are obliged to propose courses of study and to advise students who have in view one or another profession what courses they shall take. But what courses we propose and what advice we give depend over and over upon what we believe as to the practical usableness of our science. We are therefore each of us bound in conscience to face the question as well as we can, not as one of those questions which may wait upon the leisure of science, but as an always immediate question to which we can scarcely help giving daily some sort of answer to those who look to us for guidance. We are in the position of the conscientious physician who would like to wait for the instruction of another hundred years of experimental medicine but who must do as well as he can with the patient before him. For better or for worse, therefore, I shall give the conclusions which with time have come to me.

THE FAILURE OF THEORY

When a theory will not work, as so often the most promising theory will not, I believe the difficulty lies simply in the fact that the theory is not true—not true, that is, with a sufficient degree of approximation. An action is always necessarily concrete, subject not only to certain known general laws and to certain known definite conditions, but subject to the whole of reality then and there effectively present. No theory completely embraces all the conditions determining any action. Some conditions are omitted unintentionally because of ignorance. Some conditions are excluded intentionally, on the one hand as disturbances which interfere with the accuracy of experimental results, on the other hand as complications which interfere with the possibility of mathematical or logical treatment. The intentional exclusion of disturbing or complicating conditions is not a procedure which requires defense. Its defense is found in the whole history of learning, and after that in the history of the practical applications of learning. To make any progress, we must focus for certain things and be temporarily blind to environing things.

It may be, however, that in arriving at a theoretical result, either because of my ignorance, or because of the very efforts to be exact or to be logical, I shall leave out of account conditions which are not in fact insignificant, which will not be absent when my bit of theory is tried, which will be there to upset all my previsions and to bring me to confusion. My airship will not fly. In such a case, the best fortune is immediate and decisive practical trial. Decisive failure destroys our illusions, if we have them, and sets us looking for conditions which have been overlooked. Unhappily, however, decisive trial of theoretical results is often indefinitely postponed. In this case, the scholar must be of extraordinary constitution if he escape the historic disease of his kind, namely, blindness to realities which his method has not embraced.

I wish to consider two types of this illusion of the scholar. One of them, which may be called *the illusion of consistency*, is generally recognized. The other, not so generally recognized, I shall call *the illusion of precision.* I wish to show how in both cases these illusions spring directly out of the painstaking employment of methods which must be employed to discover the truth, and how, when they have risen, they render the scholar blind to certain aspects of truth which are not insignificant either in theory or in practice.

The Illusion of Consistency

I am, let us suppose, a scholar who is impressed above all things with the necessary self-consistency of the truth. Accordingly, I have spent years in developing a system of greater or less extent, which, to my mind, has the quality of complete self-consistency. I have made its consistency explicit, by stating everything in exact logical or perhaps mathematical form. Every term, every proposition or equation, every syllogism or problem is perfectly defined and the whole stands, to my mind, flawless and self-evidential. Everything in it hangs together. Everything in it can be shown to be as certain as the most certain thing in it and that thing no sane man can doubt. Here is the truth, final and clear, and here, within the field concerned, is the law for action.

Whether such a system be finally credited with great value or with small, it is sure to have certain characteristics which limit its value. Its salient merit of exact logical or mathematical consistency was bought at a price. That price was the exclusion of conditions too complicated to be dealt with by the logical or mathematical methods employed. That price was paid by Spinoza in one field and by Newton in another. The procedure requires no defense. It is necessary. There is no definition without negation.

However, a lifetime spent in developing and contemplating such a system makes it easy to forget and ignore altogether what the method has excluded. Every clear idea, as we know experimentally, makes it harder to do justice to impressions just unlike those which belong with that idea. A system of such ideas is self-protecting somewhat after the analogy of a living organism. Every item in the system is felt to be proof of and proved by all the others. Everything in the system comes to the point of attack, makes me abnormally sensitive for faint experiences of the right sort, and abnormally oblivious to salient facts of the wrong sort. In a word, there is perhaps no hypnotic agent more powerful to sharpen the sight or to dull it than a system of ideas which one has made for himself, and whose truth seems guaranteed at every turn by complete internal consistency.

Very likely this hypnotic illusion of consistency is strongest when the system concerned is believed to be all-embracing—a philosophy of God, the world, man, what not; and the illusion is the less likely to be broken because decisive trial is so difficult if not quite impossible. However, it is not simply the philosophers who, along with their systems of beliefs, develop the illusion of consistency. No doubt every man does so in a degree and men of science along with the rest. The history of science is full of examples. It is seldom that a scientist is able to do justice to facts which controvert his most important theories. For this reason there is sober truth in the cynical remark that the progress of science requires the death of scientists.

The illusion of consistency, as I have said, is very well known, for it springs out of conditions which have been legitimately and conspicuously present throughout the history of learning. And so for centuries this illusion has been notorious as a limitation of the scholar's knowledge and practical judgment.

I turn to an analogous illusion which is less generally recognized.

The Illusion of Precision

To take a typical case, let us suppose that I am not a logician but an experimental scientist. I cultivate a distrust for philosophy. I am wary of all elaborate argumentation. Logic is a trap. I have studied facts pure and simple. I have lived in the laboratory. I do nothing except with instruments of precision. I have learned how to shut out disturbing conditions with the last degree of refinement. My results are strictly quantitative. Everything has been verified over and over and is verifiable by whom you please *ad libitum*. The outcome is not poetry, not a guess, not a speculation. It is science and, within its field, it is the law for action.

It would be idle in this presence to insist upon the value of such procedures and such outcomes. The chief merit of our time lies doubtless in the fact that we have succeeded better along these lines than men ever did before. And yet directly out of the methods which science must employ there rises over and over again an illusion which stands between the scholar and the truth and which may make him a failure in practice.

Those disturbing conditions which were with infinite pains shut out may be practically insignificant. Or the scientist may take adequate account of them in a separate study. But sometimes they are not insignificant and sometimes, after having carefully shut them out of his laboratory, the scientist forgets them altogether and does not dream that they are waiting outside his laboratory door ready to take revenge when his formulae come to trial. Unhappily the necessary practical tests are often long delayed or indecisive. This is true in every field of science and there is no field of science where such delay does not permit the illusion of precision to survive.

But when the phenomena concerned are very complicated, when, for example, we confront the complexities of human nature in the individual and in society, when we attack by exact scientific method the problems of psychology, ethics, political economy, or any science dealing with human life, and thereupon undertake to tell men what to do, we have then the best possible conditions for the development of the illusion of precision.

For on the one hand it is possible in all these fields to be as precise as one will. There are methods from the older sciences to serve as analogical models. There are, if you like, instruments of the highest precision. One has only to be scrupulous, persistent, intolerant of errors. One will end by securing results which, whatever else may be true of them, are at any rate exact. All this tends to establish in the man who does it a faith which cannot be shaken. There is my machine. There is my mathematical method. There are my statistics. There is my sure concrete fact which no one can deny, which all the world may verify. There is a bit of *science* which will stand till the judgment day and take its place along with all the rest. How can there be any illusion in this? Is not this precisely the death of illusions? Is not this incoming of exact science the beginning of the end of every erroneous conception of human life?

So be it. There rises here nevertheless an illusion from which few of us altogether escape. If I would remember just what my scientific work has actually made known to me, namely, a fragment, which exists never in isolation but always in flux with innumerable other things which have not been scientifically determined, that would guard me against serious illusion—that would keep me, as a scientist, from believing or from advising or from prophesying except within the safe and narrow limits of my scientific knowledge.

But in fact it is fatally easy to forget how little I know, to forget the whole tangle of things which I have left out through ignorance or shut out in the interest of accuracy, to believe in a word that the whole complex affair from which I have painfully abstracted and defined a fragment goes on by rules laid down in my monograph.

If one wishes to see the illusion of precision in an extreme and typically clear case he can find it sometimes in a young man just become a doctor. The young man has to his credit one dissertation upon some item of human experience. That has made him an initiate. He has passed from the outside world and is one of those who may speak to the outside world with the authority of science. His work touches great affairs in education, politics, ethics, or religion. Time out of mind men have dealt with these affairs by rule of thumb, by their five wits, by what you please. The time for all that is past. This is the age of science. Let all concerned read this dissertation and govern themselves accordingly.

I wish I could say that this illusion was confined to a few unripe doctors of philosophy. In truth, the literature of the sciences dealing with human life overflows with examples, wherein men demand and expect a new education, a new politics, a new ethics, the revolution of institutions, each man assuming to speak with the authority of science, while yet no six of them could agree upon the program which science requires.

In brief, taking for granted that every sort of phenomenon admits of and requires exact scientific investigation, I am of those who believe that every bit of knowledge, so far as it is true, is actually or potentially practical. I see no reason why any pulse of consciousness which reflects any aspect of reality may not really and usefully affect action.

It is an obvious fact, indeed, that in some

cases the state of our knowledge permits us to formulate rules of procedure such that the results may be foreseen in highly accurate detail, while in other cases such precise prevision and prescription are quite impossible. Naturally the cases where this is possible lie in fields where the phenomena involved are simplest, most easily defined, most thoroughly studied, and therefore already most completely understood. These conditions are doubtless found best in the phenomena dealt with in the simpler chapters of mechanics, chemistry, etc., and are most conspicuously absent when we confront the subtle complexities of human behavior. We know how to make soap but we do not know what Shakespeare will say next.

Reflection on this obvious contrast has given rise to the doctrine that there is a difference *per se* between nature and mind such that exact theoretical and practical science is possible in the one case but not in the other. In fact, however, the line between the simple, well-understood phenomena where we have exact theoretical and practical knowledge, on the one hand, and the complex, little-understood phenomena where we must guess and fumble and grope is not at all identical with the line which divides nature and mind. Our chemistry, mechanics, physics, biology, etc., confront fields within which nearly everything remains to be done and where we can still do nothing but guess and fumble and grope.

On the other hand we are not without a body of definite verified knowledge of human nature which gives us reliable practical guidance. I can think of no reason why this theoretical and practical knowledge of human nature should not continue to grow side by side with physical science, both of them becoming with the years more comprehensive, more exact, and more useful.

Nevertheless, the life of the scholar tends to unfit him to succeed practically in any field, tends to make his advice inadequate in every field, unless his work as scholar is tested, corrected, and brought into due perspective with things outside his specialty by thoroughgoing practical experience. A lifetime spent in developing a system whose criterion of validity is its internal logical or mathematical consistency may bring about a signal advance toward a finally valid view of all truth. In like manner a lifetime spent in intelligent scientific research makes its contribution to theoretical and in the long run to practical knowledge. But never, I believe, does either of these procedures or both of them combined determine all the conditions of any action. Always some of these conditions are shut out through ignorance or for the sake of consistency or for the sake of accuracy. From these excluded conditions the eye of the scholar is holden so that he cannot see them. And when from the height of his learning he tells the foolish multitude what to do, it is not simply the multitude which replies that he also is foolish. It is over and over again the greater reality which, speaking through the event, brings him to confusion.

THE SUCCESS OF THEORY

I turn now briefly to the question, how may we mediate between abstract aspects or fragments of truth and the requirements of practice? There are two answers to this question which have weight beyond any individual opinion.

Applied Science

The first answer is given in one clear form by the higher schools of technology. The professors in these schools are in the best cases men who, after thorough training in one or another fundamental science, devote themselves to the study of concrete problems for which a practical solution is required.

It is not to be overlooked that such studies have value as contributions to scientific theory. The technical sciences are not simply borrowers from the pure sciences. They exploit new aspects of reality. They establish new facts which "stand in their own right, throw light upon the less and the more complicated aspects of reality and so do their share toward a future correlation of the sciences into science."[2] What concerns us now, however, is not the contribution of such studies to scientific theory, but the fact that such studies must be made as bridges between abstract science and practice.

If we inquire for analogous studies within the field of psychology, what showing can be made? We have for one thing a literature dealing with artificially isolated aspects of conscious life, such as will, attention, association, and the like. We have another literature dealing experimentally with functions and processes which are in themselves concrete but which in the investigations are isolated from the complex stream of life in which alone they normally occur. We have, finally, pseudoscientific literatures, phrenology, physiognomy, and the like, which are concrete enough, and

2. Bryan and Harter, *ibid.*, VI, 346.

which tell all men specifically what to do, but which science has disowned.

When we have told off these departments of our literature, comparatively little remains, and yet something remains. "Within the fields of comparative psychology, psychiatry, criminal and industrial psychology, we have pictures of the typical conduct of animals, children, melancholiacs, paranoiacs, etc., which instruct us better than unscientific popular psychology can, what to expect and what to do in dealing with individuals of these sorts."[3]

What the future will bring forth in the field of concrete psychology, whether in time the studies in this field will approach in importance the studies which now issue from the technical schools, only the future can show. For myself I have grown in the belief that in a great range of current psychological problems it is good strategy for the experimental psychologist to supplement his investigation of isolated activities and functions by the investigation of concrete activities and functions as they appear in everyday life. I believe that in this direction there lie new chapters in the history of psychology. . . .

3. *Ibid.*, p. 347.

Experience with Affairs

A second indispensable form of mediation between theory, whether abstract or concrete, and practice is found only in personal practical experience with affairs. Many scholars of course never enjoy this experience. Some never wish to enjoy it. It is easy, as we know, for a professor to become in effect a monk, living apart in his university monastery with cool and distant regard for the society from which himself and the university derive—often with childlike ignorance even of those practical affairs which his own specialty most nearly touches. If such a man does his own business well, his social isolation is socially justified. He does one thing which he can do best and all men profit by it. The practical results of such work may, in the long run, prove to be incalculably great. Faraday, Kant, or Darwin works fifty years upon a problem which seems remote. The busy public will believe anything of him except that he will ever accomplish anything practical. Yet we know very well that the ideas of such a scholar may in another fifty years quite transform both the ideas and the forms of business of the practical public.

It is equally certain, however, that learning does not effect such results except through scholars who are also men of affairs. It is the extraordinary good fortune of society to have had not a few such men. A Kelvin becomes counselor to engineers. A Lecky or a Virchow serves in Parliament. A Lowell or a White enters the diplomatic service. An Eliot becomes a university president. In such a case the scholar does not confront society with remote academic advice. With all his learning, experience, and will he grapples with men and affairs as they are. He is not there to announce principles. He is there to secure results. His principles are to be made flesh and dwell among us. His learning and his ideals throw their light about him as he works, but in the stubborn and tangled realities with which he works there is also light which in a lifetime may quite illuminate and transfigure his learning and his ideals. In a word the scholar may at a great price become a statesman. When this occurs, whether on a great scale or on a small one, whether at court or in a village school, we have at last a solution of the ancient problem of theory and practice.

For myself, I would not undervalue the psychological knowledge of the man in the street. I would try to understand those men who, without training in scientific psychology, perhaps without training in any kind of scholarship, prove that they have unusual insight into human nature and unusual success in winning men to their will. There are the politicians, the propagandists, the promoters, the peasant Stalin, the peasant Hitler, the good men and the bad, who throughout history have won men to follow them as the children followed the Pied Piper. In considering these unacademic masters of men, I would follow the example of the anthropologist who studies alien races. He does not begin or end with scorn of them. He goes to live among them. He tries to understand them, their knowledge, their skill, their failures, and their successes. So, as psychologist, I would sometimes leave my laboratory and become myself man in the street. I could become one of them if I should try to raise money, as the unacademic Scot and the unacademic Hebrew do. In that inexorable experiment, I would come upon some very obstinate realities of human nature. And I would come to realize that in winning men to give up their money, scientific psychology has, up to now, found no adequate substitute for the psychology of that Scot and that Hebrew.

Or consider Abraham Lincoln, psychologist. What was his problem and how did he meet it?

To win the war there must be guns and ships and money to pay for all. For these the President had at command engineers and financiers. There was a more urgent necessity. The President must win and hold to his purpose a decisive majority of the people. He must hold not only those who were irrevocably at one with his purpose, but also the millions who might change their minds. He must, somehow, have a correct sense of what those millions would think and do in response to his words and acts. He must know, day by day, how fast and how far those folk would follow him in his purpose to save the Union.

For a single critical instance, consider Lincoln's problem as to *when* he should issue the Emancipation Proclamation. He was urged to hurry lest England, France, and Spain should declare for the South. He was urged to wait lest millions in the border states should be driven into the arms of the South. Lincoln's problem, upon which the fate of the Union depended, was a problem of psychology —a problem of human reactions and human behaviors. The critical question was *When?* When would enough of the people be ready to support the policy of his Proclamation? This was Lincoln's inescapable psychological problem in 1862. He had no aid from any kind of systematic psychology. What we now call scientific psychology was scarcely then born. But suppose scientific psychology in 1862 had been what it is in 1940. Is there any psychologist, or anyone else, who believes that scientific psychology as it now is could have told Lincoln when to speak? Lincoln had to find his answer in his own way. He found it.

I have full faith in psychology, in its present worth and in its promise of increasing worth—both for theory and for use. The small army of those who are devoted to that science are of one spirit with the great army of those who are devoted to science as a whole. There is in all of them an irrepressible urge which nothing can stop except the destruction of civilization by war. But the sciences which deal with things began sooner and have gone farther than the sciences which deal with human nature. The science of psychology at its best is still far from having arrived at any such law as the second law of thermodynamics, and still farther from being able to tell Abraham Lincoln in a matter of major policy what to do next.

II

SCHOLAR AGAINST SCHOLAR

I PROPOSE now to look at certain hostilities which appear between scholar and scholar, especially those which have recurred age after age and which give no promise of arriving at a pacific end.

Scientist against Metaphysician

Most obvious is the hostility often found in men of science toward philosophy, of whatever brand. The astronomer De Sitter says in the Lowell Lectures of 1931: "There is nothing an orthodox physicist abhors more than metaphysics." The many scientists with this abhorrence have thought of man in search of truth as a kind of Laocoön struggling in the coils of serpents, each serpent being a different sort of metaphysics. They have held that the scholar must escape altogether from the strangling metaphysical serpents and must meet the problems which the universe presents by dividing each into many specific problems, more and more minute, down to the antennae of the paleozoic cockroach, down to the cell, the gene, the atom, the electron, always down to something which can be accurately observed and if possible measured and dealt with mathematically. Many scientists believe that in this way man in search of truth has escaped the wrong and futile way of metaphysics and has found in strict scientific method the only right way to the truth which mankind wants and needs. They are fortified in this belief by the enormous success of scientific method, especially within the past three centuries. The successes have been great, both in the pure and in the applied sciences. Especially in applied physical science, they have come in such a stream, and then in such a torrent, that even the skeptical man in the street is often convinced that the scientist has found the one right way to dependable knowledge.

The belief that metaphysics is futile and that science, as defined and pursued in the universities, is the one best way to truth has often been systematically formulated, as for example by Auguste Comte. Comte holds that mankind escaped from theological into metaphysical explanations of nature and now is escaping and must escape from metaphysics into positive science. The series of sciences, beginning with those which deal with inorganic nature and ending with those which deal with human society, provides, according to Comte, the only valid knowledge which men possess or can ever possess. There are histories of philosophy such as that by George Lewes, devoted to showing in detail that each and every system of philosophy ends in futility.

Meanwhile the philosophers by no means surrender. In every generation men of philosophic mind rise to meet every attack and parry blow with blow. In this war the defenders of philosophy gain and the abhorrers lose by the fact that many men of the greatest eminence in philosophy are eminent also in science. It is enough to name Descartes, Leibnitz, Immanuel Kant. Among later and less notable men of science who have developed comprehensive systems of philosophy one recalls Ernst Haeckel, zoölogist, contemporary and supporter of Darwin, whose monistic philosophy confidently offers a solution of all the philosophic riddles of the universe. Of the many contemporary men of science who are deeply engaged with the problems of philosophy one may name General Smuts, lately president of the British Association for the Advancement of Science, Bertrand Russell, the Nobel Prize winners Eddington and Arthur Compton, and many others. In fine, if philosophy consists of strangling serpents, there are many distinguished scientists of this day who are still involved in the coils.

THE PROBLEM OF CERTAINTY

I propose now to look at a single one of the problems of philosophy with which scientists and philosophers alike are concerned and about which there has been never-finished war. The question is: How, if at all, can we arrive at knowledge of anything which is certainly true? I propose to consider three of the answers which have been made.

First: We know nothing with certainty. We know nothing at all of which the opposite may not be proved equally probable.

Second: The universe is in part knowable and known, in part unknowable and unknown or known only by supernatural means.

Third: The essential truth about the universe we can and do know.

I shall confine my consideration to these three answers. I shall deal with them simply as historical facts, not to assail or defend any of them but to look at them as nearly as possible as they are understood by their advocates. In the end I shall, as in duty bound, state my own belief.

SKEPTICS AGAINST SCIENCE AND PHILOSOPHY

First I shall look at those persons who, troubled by the confusions and contradictions in their experience, conclude that we can know nothing at all with certainty, through philosophy, or through science, or by any other means. They renounce the fight to understand the universe or any part of it. They say that the fight for knowledge ends always and everywhere in failure. These radical doubters about the possibility of certain and trustworthy knowledge are never numerous but are always present throughout the history of civilization. Well-known groups appeared late in the history of Greece, who attacked the whole majestic procession of Greek scientists and philosophers. Greek scholars, beginning in the seventh century before the Christian era, had sought to escape from mythological into natural explanations of the universe. One after another through successive centuries they wrestled with problems which have ever since challenged the interest of men. They had in various special fields—mathematics, astronomy, geography, medicine, etc.—arrived at results based upon observation of facts which are still recorded with respect in the history of science. Euclid, Archimedes,

Hippocrates are not forgotten. The Greek scholars dared further. They sought to understand the universe as a whole. Each in his turn conceived a philosophy of all existence. The earlier ones sought only to discern the nature of material things. The later ones raised every question about nature, mind, and God; about the true method of knowledge; about ethics, politics, and religion—every problem with which human beings are concerned. Through seven or eight hundred years Greek scholars fared forth into the unknown in search of its innermost secret. One must look with wonder at this astonishing exhibition of human courage and persistence, even if one should conclude that the whole endeavor ended in failure and futility.

This was just the conclusion of those rebels against science and philosophy who appeared among the Greeks in the last three centuries before the Christian era. They observed that none of the philosophers had secured general acceptance of his philosophy against the others. The philosophers had not agreed:

As to the constitution of matter,

Or whether matter is discrete or continuous,

Or whether the universe is of one substance or many,

Or whether the universe is governed by mind, necessity, or chance.

There were other differences no less profound. So the extreme rebels said: All the philosophers are wrong. They all strive to know what nobody can know. All the scientists are wrong. All the instruments of knowledge and all the methods of knowledge are deceptive. We cannot trust our senses. It is notorious that they constantly deceive us. We cannot trust our reasoning. We are the victims of our logic. We know nothing at all which is not presently upset by an equally probable opposite. The only wise man is the man who gives up the impossible quest for the mirage called truth and who seeks for himself the peace of imperturbability. I quote from the Cambridge University lectures on modern science:

"This phenomenalism is, I think, the best way to face the difficulties which some men have professed to see in the science founded by Galileo. As a map or a chart represents the surface of the land in a systematic but conventional manner, so science represents the reality which underlies it. The map or chart does not show the land as we see it, like a picture or photograph, but it is consistent within itself, and it can be used safely and confidently as a guide by travellers. So the model which science constructs is self-consistent; it can be used as a guide to practical life, and as a means of predicting future physical events with a high degree of probability. But science, dealing only with these models and forms in which we group the relations between phenomena, does not within its own realm reveal or even touch reality. We are perhaps returning towards Plato's old theory of ideas. When we discover scientific relations—Laws of Nature, shall we say—they connect together ideal forms, and it is between such concepts that the relations hold. Plato argued, as I said at the beginning, that such ideal forms were the only reality, and thus arrived at idealistic realism. To us the models are the subject-matter of science—scientific, but not metaphysical or fundamental reality. Between them scientific determinism holds good. The error comes in when that determinism is transferred to the unknown concrete reality from which those concepts have been extracted.

"The whole mystery that mankind has to face undoubtedly involves the problem of the nature of reality, but that is a metaphysical not a scientific problem. The fact that a consistent model of Nature can be put together by science is a valid metaphysical argument in favour of the view that some reality, corresponding in some close way to the model science makes, lies hidden beneath phenomena, but science does not directly reveal that reality as we used to think.

"In the laboratory, as in practical life, there is no room or time for philosophic doubt, but in periods of reflection it is well to remember the purely conceptual nature of science when based solely on its own inductions." Sir William C. Dampier, "From Aristotle to Galileo," *Background to Modern Science,* pp. 44–46.

"I have told you, as best I can, something of what we have learnt in the last forty years. I will end by expressing a hope—not unmingled with doubt—that not too much of what I have been saying will be upset in the next forty years." Sir Arthur Eddington, "Forty Years of Astronomy," *Background to Modern Science,* p. 142.

MONTAIGNE AND PASCAL

The Greek skeptics were not the last of their race. One recalls Montaigne. That mighty contemporary of Shakespeare and Cervantes looked at the race of men as profoundly as they did and found nothing universally accepted by men as true. He said the fact that we differ proves that things are as we think them.

One recalls Pascal, a successor to Galileo, forerunner of Newton. After rising to heights of achievement in mathematics and physics excelled only by Newton, while still a young man and in the midst of his scientific triumphs, Pascal abandoned science. Not at all because of attacks from the enemies of science. Pascal abandoned science because he concluded that the quest of science is forever futile. He has to his credit a remarkable list of achievements in plane geometry, conic sections, the beginnings of calculus, the mathematics of probability, hydrodynamics, and so on and so on. A high authority says: "After the lapse of more than two hundred years, we can still point to much in exact science which is absolutely his and we can indicate infinitely more which is his by inspiration." In a weighty consensus as to the thousand greatest men of history, a work edited by an eminent living scientist, Pascal is placed with the hundred greatest men and with the ten greatest men of science who have ever lived.

But this man while still young, winning for physics and mathematics one great victory after another, suddenly quit. To paraphrase

Kipling, so far as the affairs of science were concerned, Pascal died. He tells us why.

Science, he decided, can never solve the problem which nature sets. "I am in terrible ignorance of all things," he said. "I see nothing but infinities on every side. All this visible world is but an imperceptible point in the ample bosom of nature. In vain we extend our conceptions beyond imaginable spaces. . . . The universe is an infinite sphere whose center is everywhere and whose circumference is nowhere. . . . And if one turns to what is most minute, I will picture to him not only the visible universe but the conceivable immensity of nature in the compass of this abbreviation of an atom."

THE CERTAINTIES OF THE NEWTONIAN UNIVERSE

However, it will be said, all that skepticism of science came before Newton; since Newton science has achieved certainties which would seem to make doubt of them impossible for intelligent men. Turn then to Newton.

On April 21, 1686, the astronomer Edmund Halley

read to the Royal Society his Discourse Concerning Gravitation and its Properties, in which he stated that his worthy countryman Mr.

Isaac Newton has an incomparable treatise of motion almost ready for the press and that the law of the inverse square is the principle on which Mr. Newton has made out all the phenomena of the celestial motions so easily and naturally that its truth is past dispute.

Imagine a meeting of the Royal Society on April 21, 1886, in commemoration of the two hundredth anniversary of that truly epoch-making announcement. The principal address on that occasion would be made by an eminent successor of Sir Isaac Newton. We may safely surmise the principal topics of the commemorative address: brief recognition of the ancient forerunners of Newton, such as Euclid, for Newton was indebted to Euclid; more extended recognition of his modern predecessors, Kepler, Copernicus, Galileo, and others worthy to be named with them, not omitting the illustrious renegade to science Pascal; then a résumé of the work which gave Newton his high place among the world's men of science; finally a review of the work of Newton's great successors down to 1886, the whole culminating in the vast and solid structure which has been called the Newtonian universe.

On that day some may have remembered the Greek skeptics, their distrust of all theories of the universe, and their surrender of the quest for any finally valid knowledge of anything. Against that background of distrust and surrender stood the confidence of the Royal Society and all other scientific societies of 1886 in the indestructible stability of the Newtonian universe. One may say without reserve that never before did any system of belief developed by human intelligence have the assent of so many civilized men. It was sustained by the whole body of scientists, with here and there a deep-seeing questioner such as Clerk-Maxwell. It was accepted by the whole body of enlightened men. A central law of the Newtonian universe was held to be so certain that things were said to be "as certain as the law of gravitation." The confidence of physicists late in the last century in the stability of the classical physics found expression in a statement by one of the greatest of them, the Nobel Prize winner Professor Albert Michelson:

While it is never safe to affirm that the future of physical science has no marvels in store even more astonishing than those of the past, it seems probable that most of the grand underlying principles have been firmly established and that further advances are to be sought chiefly in the rigorous application of those principles to all the phenomena which come under our notice.

It is here that the science of measurement shows its importance—where quantitative results are more to be desired than qualitative work. An eminent physicist has remarked that the future truths of physical science are to be looked for in the sixth place of decimals.[1]

In a recent article Professor Millikan has written in high praise of his former colleague, Professor Michelson,[2] ranking him as one of the three Americans who have made the most important contributions to physics. Michelson, he says, bitterly reproached himself for making the statement which I have just quoted. Yet it appeared in two successive volumes of the *Annual Register* of the University of Chicago and no doubt met with the general assent of the physicists of that day.

THE UNCERTAINTIES OF THE NEWTONIAN UNIVERSE

But alas for human certainties. At the moment when the eminent physicist wrote those lines things were beginning to happen within the Newtonian universe. Not as a result of assaults from without. There was in those days war against some scientific theories, especially the theory of evolution, but no one made war

1. *Annual Register,* University of Chicago Press, p. 283, 1896–97. Also 1897–98.
2. *Scientific Monthly,* Jan., 1939.

upon the law of gravitation. Nonscientists did not make war upon the mathematical sciences, as they were taught throughout the world in the closing years of the last century. What has happened to the Newtonian universe has been effected by the most eminent men who have wrought at its center. Only they can say what has happened. Few others, even among scientists in other fields, can even be made to understand just what has happened. Professor Sumner, biologist of the Scripps Institute of Oceanography, writes: "How many persons have the faintest idea what the name of Einstein stands for in the history of science? How many persons, indeed how many scientists, are even capable of learning this, try as they may? One may try, but he loses the trail suddenly, after sinking deeper into what seems to him a bog of paradoxes and *non sequiturs.*" Professor Sumner does not deny the truth of the new physics. He faces its recondite mathematics as one might face the recondite metaphysics of medieval arguments for the Trinity —without understanding.

However, laymen are assured of two things: first, that the changes in physical theory within this century are very great and fundamental, and second, that they have not stopped—they go on and on. On the first point I select from the many available statements by eminent physicists one by the Nobel Prize winner, Professor Millikan:

> The historian of the future will estimate the past thirty years as the most extraordinary in the history of the world up to the present, in the number and the fundamental character of the discoveries in physics to which it has given birth; and in the changes brought about by these discoveries in man's conception as to the nature of the physical world in which he lives. . . . Of the six basic principles which at the end of the nineteenth century acted as the police officers to keep the physical world running in orderly fashion, there is not one the universal validity of which has not been recently questioned by serious and competent physicists, while most of them have been definitely proved to be subject to exceptions.[3]

Professor Millikan lists six basic principles of nineteenth-century physics which have been questioned or proved to be subject to exceptions:

1. The conservation of the chemical elements.
2. Conservation of mass.

3. Robert A. Millikan, "The Last Fifteen Years of Physics," vol. I, chap. v, pp. 115–116, *Science and the New Civilization* (1926).

3. Conservation of energy.

4. Conservation of momentum.

5. The principle underlying Maxwell's electrodynamics.

6. Entropy or the second law of thermodynamics.

The changes have not stopped. I quote from the introduction to the Lowell Lectures of 1931 by Professor de Sitter, astronomer at Leiden:

> In the same year, 1914, Einstein's *Entwurf einer verallgemeinerten Relativitätstheorie und Theorie der Gravitation* was published. I need not call back to your mind how many controversies, not always conducted in a dignified manner, this theory has elicited. In November 1915 the theory was completed and began its triumphal march through the world, gaining its final victory as early as 1919 by the results of the English eclipse expeditions. It seemed at first as if here at least a safe harbour had been reached, where we could rest and quietly sort out the treasures that the venturesome voyage into new regions had brought us. But presently the further development went in unexpected directions, and brought most strange and paradoxical results.
>
> In the domain of atomic physics the confusion has been still worse. About the same time, now nearly twenty years ago, Bohr's theory was

developed. The quantum theory assumed a new aspect and soon rose to high esteem. But this glory did not last long. The theory of fifteen years ago is now an historical curiosity, known under the name of the "classical quantum theory." It has been successsively replaced by the "new quantum theory," the theory of matrices, wave mechanics, each stranger and more paradoxical than its predecessor. What used to be the most fundamental concepts of physical science, determinism and causality, are called into doubt, the foundations of science appear to be shaking, and it seems as if the whole building were tottering.[4]

The startling rapidity with which these great changes in fundamental theory have come gives rise to the suggestion that we may have a succession of Nobel Prize winners, each of whom will win the prize by overthrowing what his predecessor won the prize by establishing.

Bertrand Russell writes:

The world according to them [the scientists] is a more higgledy-piggledy and haphazard affair than it was thought to be. And they know much less about it than was thought to be known by their predecessors in the eighteenth and nineteenth centuries. Perhaps the scientific

4. W. de Sitter, *Kosmos,* chap. i, p. 4.

skepticism of which Eddington is an exponent may lead in the end to the collapse of the scientific era, just as the theological skepticism of the Renaissance has led gradually to the collapse of the theological era. I suppose that machines will survive the collapse of science, just as parsons have survived the collapse of theology, but in the one case as in the other they will cease to be viewed with reverence and awe. Perhaps this is not to be regretted.[5]

And again:

While science as the pursuit of power becomes increasingly triumphant, science as the pursuit of truth is being killed by a skepticism which the skill of the men of science has generated.[6]

Professor Bridgman writes:

The revolution that now confronts us arises from the recent discovery of new facts, the only interpretation of which is that our conviction that nature is understandable and subject to law arose from the narrowness of our horizons, and that if we sufficiently extend our range, we shall find that nature is intrinsically and in its elements neither understandable nor subject to law. . . . The physicist thus finds himself in a world from which the bottom has dropped clean

5. Bertrand Russell, "The Twilight of Sciences," *Century Magazine* (July, 1929), pp. 314–315.
6. *The Scientific Outlook* (1931), p. 100.

out; as he penetrates deeper and deeper, it eludes him and fades away by the highly unsportsmanlike device of just becoming meaningless. . . . But doubtless by far the most important effect of this revolution will not be on the scientist, but on the man in the street. The immediate effect will be to let loose a veritable intellectual spree of licentious and debauched thinking.[7]

Professor Eddington, Nobel winner of Cambridge University, describes the search for reality in the table upon which he writes. To common sense it is just a solid wooden table. Scientists of fifty years ago were unanimous in the certainty that the table is in reality an aggregation of atoms in rapid motion, several kinds of atoms, none convertible into any other kind, all forever indestructible. But within fifty years there has been a change of belief about atoms. The atom appears not to be an indestructible bullet but a cosmos, whose infinitely smaller element is known as the electron. And what is an electron, this item of reality of which the table and the universe are made? Professor Eddington says: "The electron is we know not what, doing we know not what."

7. P. Bridgman, "Skepticism, Pragmatism, and Truth," *Harper's,* March, 1929.

Professor Smith, philosopher, University of Chicago, writes that philosophy and science both have failed.

> Science restored the hunger and hope of mankind for truth. It has been all but universally believed that it would produce a key to the other mysteries of the universe as it has opened a sure lever to turn natural energies to human aid. Alas, it cannot appease the hunger which it has engendered. It cannot satisfy the hope it has raised. We have asked for truth. We have been given gadgets.

I imagine Pascal come back to earth to attend a meeting of physicists and mathematicians today. They receive him with the highest honor. I hear him inquire gravely what they have done in the years since he went away. They tell him what has happened to the stuff of which they thought the world was made, the atoms which in 1890 they mistakenly thought to be certain and final. They tell him that many of them no longer believe in the two laws formerly supposed to be most certain of all—Newton's law of gravitation and the law of causation. One notable physicist, expressing the view of many, tells him that "nature is intrinsically and in its elements neither understandable nor subject to law."

When Pascal hears this story, I imagine him saying: "After near three hundred years you are exactly where I was when I gave up. In the most minute atom of nature you still find, as I said you would, a new unknown abyss. Your universe is still, as I said it was, an infinite sphere whose center is everywhere and whose circumference is nowhere. You are still, you men of science, strangled in a tangle of knots which can never be untied."

THE SKEPTICS TOWARD SCIENCE AND PHILOSOPHY ARE A FAMILY OF MINDS

I believe that I am justified in regarding those who despair of valid knowledge, whether by science or by philosophy, as a family of minds. The world which they confront is not more complicated, more harassed with unsolved riddles, than is the world faced by the rest of mankind. But the rest of mankind do not surrender. Most men face the problems of knowledge as they face the problem of keeping alive. Through all dangers and through all sufferings most men fight to live. And through all the inexplicable exigencies of experience most men strive to see something intelligible which they call common sense or science or philosophy and which they trust as true. But there are those who give up the fight to keep alive. And there are those who give up the fight to understand the universe or any part of it. It isn't a special kind of experience which leads such men to despair of valid knowledge. It is a special kind of disposition with which they meet experience that accounts for the always-present Skeptic Family of Minds.

FEW SCIENTISTS BECOME SKEPTICS TOWARD SCIENCE

Most scientists, including most of those like Einstein who have wrought the revolution, do not quit. Science, pure and applied, goes on just as it went on regardless of Pyrrho or Pascal or any other scientific doubters of science. Many scientists, perhaps most of them, simply ignore the doubters and the doubts and go on each with his own quest. Others have an answer.

THE CONSISTENT AGNOSTIC TOWARD METAPHYSICS

One answer is that we do see much that is true, but cannot see or at any rate have not yet seen the ultimate realities which underlie what we see. One who has expressed this view is Albert Einstein. The first chapter of his recent *Evolution of Physics* is entitled "The

Rise of the Mechanical View." The second chapter is entitled "The Decline of the Mechanical View." In the first chapter[8] he traces the development of the mechanistic theory of the universe from Galileo to the end of the nineteenth century. In the second chapter he describes its collapse. He writes:

In our short view of the principal physical ideas we have met some unsolved problems, have come upon difficulties and obstacles which discourage the attempts to formulate a uniform and consistent view of all the phenomena of the external world. . . . Our knowledge is now wider and more profound than that of the physicists of the nineteenth century, but so are our doubts and difficulties. . . . But what is the medium through which light spreads and what are its mechanical properties? There is no hope of reducing the optical phenomena to the mechanical ones before this question is answered. But the difficulties in solving this problem are so great that we have to give up the mechanical view as well. . . . The great mystery story is still unsolved. We cannot even be sure that it has a final solution. The reading has already given us much; it has taught us the rudiments of the language of nature; it has enabled us to understand many of the clews and has been a source of joy and excitement in the oftentimes painful

8. p. 57.

advance of science. But we realize that in spite of all the volumes read and understood, we are still far from a complete solution if indeed such a thing exists at all.

Although new and revolutionary physical theories have led many present-day physicists into the abysses of metaphysical disputation concerning determinism and free will, Einstein withholds judgment. For him the real cause of all events is still an unsolved mystery.

The view of Sir Isaac Newton as to a mechanistic universe is often misunderstood. Newton's *Principia* is assumed to provide a mechanistic explanation for all that can occur in the universe. Newton made no such presumptuous claim. The real cause of every event he affirmed is in God. One finds no such affirmation in Einstein. But these two giants of science agree in their view that with our normal powers of knowing we do not know the reality which underlies phenomena and do not know the real cause of any event. Charles Darwin is a third very great scientist who consistently refrains from assuming that what he has observed entitles him to be dogmatic about what he has not observed. "Darwin's own writings," says Professor Whitehead, "are for all time a model of refusal to go beyond the direct evidence, and of careful retention of every possible hypothesis. But those virtues are not so conspicuous in his followers, and still less in his camp-followers."

Among others who have shown a like reticence is Professor Henry Fairfield Osborn, paleontologist, who writes: "Personally I am strongly of the opinion that the laws of life like the ultimate laws of physics may eventually prove to be beyond analysis."[9]

THE INCONSISTENT AGNOSTIC TOWARD METAPHYSICS

There are, however, very many scientists who begin by saying that science deals only with that which has been observed and then immediately assume that the unobserved universe is like the part which has been observed. This is the story of the blind men, each of whom touched one part of the elephant. Each says that he knows only what he touches but each is sure that the whole elephant is like the part that he has touched. Now the competent scientist has gone far beyond the blind man in his knowledge about the elephant. He has seen and has correlated a vast body of phenomena concerning trunk, tail, tusks, organs, and tissues, and whatever he can by any de-

9. *Impressions of Great Naturalists,* p. 65.

vice observe. But when he stands upon the outermost frontier of what he and others have definitely experienced, will he stop there? Einstein, Newton, Darwin, and others do seem consistently to stop there. But many scientists, like most men who are not scientists, seem driven by a compelling urge to believe that what we know by experience holds true beyond what we know by experience. Not only so, we become dogmatic and hold that nothing in the unknown world can break through and upset our certainties. Most of us are brothers to the blind men.

One such brother to the blind men was Herbert Spencer, eminent scholar and philosopher of the last century. The first chapters in his series of volumes on science and philosophy are devoted to the Unknowable. "In all directions," he writes, "the scientist's investigations bring him face to face with an insoluble enigma. The scientist more than any other truly knows that in its ultimate essence nothing can be known." However, there is a knowable universe: "After concluding that we cannot know the ultimate essence of that which is manifested to us, there arise the questions: What is it that we know? In what sense do we know it? And in what consists our highest knowledge of it?" What Herbert

Spencer was sure he knew included the indestructibility of matter, the continuity of motion, and other principles of physics, all grounded in the principle of the persistence of force. Spencer held that these principles are proved true not only by verified experience but also because they are necessities of thought, their opposites being inconceivable. From them he derived his law of universal evolution and dissolution, which governed all the changes that occur in the universe as a whole or in any part thereof. "The entire procession of things as displayed in the visible universe is analogous to the entire procession of things displayed in the smallest aggregates," he writes. "There is suggested the conception of a past during which there have been successive evolutions analogous to that which is now going on and a future during which successive other such evolutions may go on, ever the same in principle but never the same in concrete results."

Now if a man knows that, if he knows with certainty all that can occur from everlasting to everlasting, what more would he know if he knew the Unknowable? When he conceived his majestic procession of universes marching out of eternity into eternity in docile obedience to his law, Spencer was just another blind man, confident that the whole troupe of elephants was like the part of one that he touched.

I turn for further illustration to scientists of our day. De Sitter writes in his Lowell Lectures:

Strictly speaking, every assertion about what has not been observed is outside of physics and belongs to metaphysics, and although there is nothing an orthodox physicist abhors more than metaphysics, still he has no hesitation at all in believing that his laws are universal and that the phenomena continue to happen according to them just the same when nobody is looking. And since it would be impossible to prove that they do not, he is fully entitled to his belief.

Such a man is part of the time agnostic toward the unobserved world and part of the time metaphysician. As agnostic he says that he knows only what he has seen or touched. As metaphysician he holds that what he has seen and touched tells him the nature of the unseen reality. Each man is in contact with one part of the elephant. Each carries across the line his belief about the whole elephant and there they meet in conflict, these men who abhor and denounce metaphysics, each with a confident metaphysics of his own.

James Ward[10] says that the agnosticism which disavows a knowledge of ultimate reality often covers a belief that physical matter is the only reality. I will add that the same disavowal is associated with every sort of belief as to the nature of reality, including in many belief in mind or spirit or a personal God. That was true of Pascal, who renounced physical science to pursue otherwise his way to spiritual reality in which he believed. It was true of many church fathers as, for example, Tertullian, who renounced the search for truth by way of the intellect and proclaimed his faith in the well-known expression: *Credo quia absurdum est*. It was true of the Apostle Paul. He had a systematic philosophy of the universe. He did not renounce it. But he said: "For we know in part, and we prophesy in part. But when that which is perfect is come, then that which is in part shall be done away." Yet underneath all was his assured belief that "God is above all, through all, and in you all." Perhaps the most universal philosophy can be expressed in these two sentences: "I do not know the ultimate truth. But I am sure of what it is. It is *this*." Each man's *this* comes out of his most profound disposition.

10. *Naturalism and Agnosticism*, pp. 206 ff.

THE METAPHYSICIANS

Come now to those who avow that we can and that we do, either by philosophy or by science, know what is real in the universe. But those who make this avowal do not agree as to the answer. When you take a first look at the history of philosophy or of science, the answers to the question as to what is certainly true seem to be a crisscross toward every point of the compass. But a first look at anything is never enough. Another and longer look reveals certain main types of answer which come down continuously century after century.

I select for illustration two such lines continuing from the beginning of organized knowledge until now in unbroken opposition to each other, the one affirming, the other denying, the reality of mind in man and in the universe.

ANCIENT AND MODERN MATERIALISTS

First, then, the materialists. The history of materialism may be told in three chapters. First, the materialism of the Greeks, which foreshadowed all that followed in that way of belief. Second, the deeply based mechanistic theory of the universe developed in the three centuries following Galileo. Third, the metaphysical behaviorism of recent psychology.

Goethe has written: "*Die Einbildung ist die Vorschule des Denkens*"—Imagination is the preparatory school of thought. So those astonishing Greeks foreshadowed almost every modern theory of science and philosophy. This is plainly the case with Greek materialism, which had its culmination in Democritus in the fifth century B.C. Lange in his monumental *History of Materialism* says that Democritus must be numbered among the greatest of the thinkers of antiquity.

Lange, following Zeller's masterly study of Democritus, writes: "Materialism stood complete as the first perfectly clear and consequent theory of all phenomena." On the basis of scrupulous examination of the texts Lange summarizes the atomism of Democritus in the following six statements:

I. Out of nothing arises nothing: nothing that is can be destroyed. All change is only combination and separation of atoms.

II. Nothing happens by chance, but everything through a cause and of necessity.

III. Nothing exists but atoms and empty space: all else is only opinion.

IV. The atoms are infinite in number, and of endless variety of form. In the eternal fall through infinite space, the greater, which fall more quickly, strike against the lesser, and the lateral movements and vortices that thus arise are the commencement of the formation of worlds. Innumerable worlds are formed and perish successively and simultaneously.

V. The variety of all things is a consequence of the variety of their atoms in number, size, figure, and arrangement: there is no qualitative difference of atoms. They have no "internal conditions": and act on each other only by pressure or collision.

VI. The soul consists of fine, smooth, round atoms, like those of fire. These atoms are the most mobile, and by their motion, which permeates the whole body, the phenomena of life are produced.[11]

The atom of Democritus gave place to the atom of Dalton and the atom of Dalton has given way in part to the atom as now conceived. But through all the changes there has persisted in the belief of many the view of Democritus that nothing exists but indestructible particles of matter. "Of the great principles underlying the materialism of all time," says Lange, "one only is lacking in Democritus, and that is the abolition of all teleology within man or within the universe."

11. Friedrich A. Lange, *History of Materialism,* I, 19–28, E. C. Thomas, translator.

Materialism after Galileo fitted in with a far larger and always growing body of accurately observed facts in the field of the physical sciences and with the development of the mechanistic theory of nature. Einstein writes:

The great achievements of mechanics in all its branches, its striking success in the development of astronomy, the application of its ideas to problems apparently different and nonmechanical in character, all these things contributed to the belief that it *is* possible to describe all natural phenomena in terms of simple forces between unalterable objects. Throughout the two centuries following Galileo's time such an endeavor, conscious or unconscious, is apparent in nearly all scientific creation. This was clearly formulated by Helmholtz about the middle of the nineteenth century:

"Finally, therefore, we discover the problem of physical, material science to be to refer natural phenomena back to unchangeable attractive and repulsive forces whose intensity depends wholly upon distance. The solubility of this problem is the condition of the complete comprehensibility of nature.

"Thus the line of development of science is determined and follows strictly a fixed course. And its vocation will be ended as soon as the reduction of natural phenomena to simple forces is complete and the proof given that this is the only reduction of which the phenomena are capable."

The mechanistic theory of nature became thus for many a scientifically established certainty which included all reality in man or anywhere in the universe.

The certainties of the mechanist are no longer certain. A large and increasing group of physicists holds that the mechanistic theory which culminated in the nineteenth century has collapsed. Einstein expresses this view in the statement that the great mystery story of nature is still unsolved.

But materialistic theory has survived the revolution in physics. It is a surprising fact that, while many physicists have been led by their studies away from the mechanistic interpretation of nature, many psychologists have moved vigorously toward that theory as applied to human behavior. The materialistic psychologist of today favors a complete explanation of all that occurs in human behavior by strictly physical causes, excluding conscious mind or purpose as having any effective reality. I have been assured that metaphysical behaviorism is dead. I have been quite unable to see the difference between a metaphysical and a nonmetaphysical behaviorist, both of whom assume to know that mind is not a real force in behavior. However that may be, materialistic theory in one form or another was perhaps never more in evidence and never more influential than it is today. Materialists have as a matter of course exercised their right to teach what they believe and fight against views which they hold to be false. The zeal of the French materialists Helvetius and La Mettrie in the eighteenth century and the German materialists of the nineteenth century, such as Moleschott and Büchner and Haeckel, has not been excelled by the missionaries of any religion. Their fight against the church and their substitution of what may be called a religion and morality founded upon materialism found a great and eagerly receptive audience, especially among the rising proletariat. Haeckel's booklet entitled *The Riddle of the Universe* had an enormous circulation and was used as a textbook by labor unions. As a single sufficient example of the influence of materialism upon great populations may be cited the official atheism of Soviet Russia.

Materialism has, I believe, never had a more powerful instrument of propaganda than present-day materialistic psychology. Materialistic physics which is now practically obsolete sought to eliminate mind and purpose from the universe by showing that physical events can be otherwise completely accounted for. Materialistic psychology undertakes to eliminate mind and purpose from man by providing complete explanation of all that occurs in human beings by physical causes without intervention of mind or purpose. Since psychologists are found in all the universities, colleges, teacher-training schools, and many high schools, and many of them teach that there is no such reality as mind, soul, or effective purpose, they are in a position to inculcate this belief far and wide among all the people. The most zealous missionary for any cause could not ask for a more powerful means of propagating his faith.

MATERIALISTS, ANCIENT AND MODERN, ARE ONE FAMILY OF MINDS

I am led to regard materialists, the ancient and the modern, as one family of minds, because as fast as one materialistic theory dies another is born. Every historic materialistic philosophy has in fact collapsed. Those philosophies have been abandoned partly, no doubt, because of searching criticism from their opponents, but chiefly because their advocates have discovered their inadequacies. That, says Hegel, is the way every inadequate theory breaks down. It may stand up against attacks from without, but when its advocates push their theory to the limit as an explanation of the universe, they discover its inadequacies and give it up. That, we are assured, is what has happened to the mechanistic theory of the universe. It broke down in the hands of its friends. It broke down as one physicist and mathematician after another felt compelled by accumulating evidence to give it up. We are assured that metaphysical behaviorism in psychology has met a like fate. But the materialistic mind does not die. When solid wood dissolves into atoms and atoms into electrons and electrons maybe into something still farther from what can be seen or touched, there is a kind of mind which is sure that that most remote item of reality must be something essentially like the solid wood. The men of this temperament, disposition, and habit of explaining the world, I feel justified in calling the Materialistic Family of Minds. Observe, I do not assail this race of men. I would look at them. I would if possible understand them. In the end I must of course say what I think of their philosophy of the universe.

ANCIENT AND MODERN IDEALISTS

Consider now in contrast the unbroken succession of those who believe that the central fact in man and in the universe is mind. Over against Greek Democritus I select for illustration Greek Aristotle.

It is the distinction of Aristotle that he was both scientist and philosopher. As scientist he knew well the not inconsiderable contributions to science of his predecessors, such as Pythagoras. Aristotle was himself a scientist, in the sense now recognized by the universities. No other man in the history of the world was a more indefatigable student of facts than he. His studies covered as nearly as possible all fields of inorganic nature, of plant and animal and human life. He studied and catalogued many plants and animals. The son of a physician, he dissected the bodies of animals and men. He wrote a treatise on psychology. He wrote profoundly on ethics and on logic, works which are alive in university classrooms today. He studied in detail the constitutions of many states such as Athens, and present-day study of political science begins with Aristotle. He wrote on the forms of literary art, and his writings are basic in the literary criticism of all later times down to the present.

Aristotle, like all great men, has suffered from unintelligent subservience and from unintelligent hostility. Many scholars came to believe that whatever Aristotle said was infallibly true. His profound judgments on the drama came to be regarded as iron laws to which artists must submit. So then Aristotle was fought, has been fought by scholar and by artist, by Molière and Lessing and Francis Bacon. Bacon performed an indispensable service when he fought Aristotle, or rather an Aristotelianism which in his day looked to the syllogism rather than to facts for a knowledge of nature. It is amusing that Bacon, who was not at all a scientific student of nature, should denounce Aristotle, who was. Scientists generally, including Bacon's scientific contemporaries, such as Harvey, discoverer of the circulation of the blood, have pointed out that Bacon did not use and did not understand the methods by which scientists work. Nevertheless, Bacon did his important part in emancipating the world from a pseudo-Aristotle.

Following his scientific studies, Aristotle proceeded to the development of a philosophy. As philosopher he sought with characteristic thoroughness to know the work of his predecessors. One may say that everything before Aristotle comes to some kind of recognition in him. There is mysticism in Aristotle, such as came to Greece from Asia, such as was found in the Greek secret mysteries, such as is found in Pythagoras and Plato. On the other hand, Aristotle knew and judged the austere reasoning of his Greek predecessors, including again and especially Plato, with whom he had on the whole more likeness than difference.

Having thus thoroughly examined the philosophies of his predecessors, as every major philosopher essays to do, Aristotle developed his own system of metaphysics. I select from his metaphysics that in it which stands in clearest contrast with the materialism of Democritus.

Does Aristotle deny or ignore what Democritus and all of us call matter? He does not. In Aristotle, matter may be said to be a residence of force, a force which works according to a plan, a force which works toward a purpose.

It is obvious that when a man makes anything like bread, or a coat, or a house, we have force working on a plan toward the fulfillment of a purpose. Aristotle held that everywhere throughout the universe there is the same fact—force acting on a plan, toward the fulfillment of purpose. The dust underfoot is not dead. There is indwelling force; there is indwelling organization; and the dust embodies purposes which lie beyond its own.

We must not read into a writer what was known only after his time. But it is a mark of the greatest thinkers that what is discovered later falls into place within their theories. Thus I have heard an eminent mathematician say that the calculus of Newton and Leibnitz contained in germ vast mathematical developments which they did not foresee.

Let me say here that nothing more impresses me with the fundamental rationality of the universe than the fact that what one living being does becomes an essential contribution to a purpose which lies far beyond its own. Thus, as Darwin has shown, the earthworm, working from its own inner urge, prepares the soil for the uses of human beings who appear on the earth millions of years later. Or again, the mathematical insight of a Newton is a small part of a vast arc which stretches far beyond even his amazing mathematical mind.

So Aristotle's theory welcomes the modern discovery that the seeming dead dust has in it inconceivably great intra-atomic energy. It welcomes the modern view that the seeming amorphous dust is not amorphous, but in its molecules, atoms, electrons has inconceivably complicated organization. Again, Aristotle did not foresee the theory of evolution as developed within the past century, but his theory welcomes it, for he did recognize the ascending stadia from seeming amorphous matter through plant life and animal life to the human individual and human society, and studied them with the ardor and method of the scientist. Aristotle's theory welcomes the view that the movements of beings ascending from dust to man are progressively more and more determined by resident forces, which at the same time are conscious forces.

Aristotle's philosophy may seem to be a kind of pantheism or panpsychism, but it is not. He conceives that the organizing, purposeful force which is in all things and in all men also transcends all things and all men. That is, the formative, purposeful force is transcendent mind, transcendent God. Aristotle might have said with Paul: "God who is above all, through all, and in you all," but with the fundamental difference that he did not conceive God as personal.

Now, partly from Aristotle and partly through him from his predecessors, there has flowed down through the centuries of time a great gulf stream of influence. It appears in the later Jewish and Saracenic philosophers, in Christian and non-Christian philosophers, in the system of Thomas Aquinas, whose *Summa* Henry Adams calls a comprehensive approach to the mind of the Middle Ages. Aristotle appears as a fundamental and recognized force in the idealism of Hegel and of other major philosophers of his type. His conceptions appear in those modern biologists who find themselves unable to explain what occurs in the processes of living beings and the evolution of living forms by chance or by mechanism, and are driven to conclude that some kind of force acting on some kind of plan is necessary to account for the facts observed in their laboratories. As a clock is both mechanical and a teleological system—each part of the mechanism having its purpose in relation to the whole—so it has been held by some biologists that the animal body is a mechanical system which is also everywhere in its functional adaptations a teleological system. Professor Pflüger, former editor of the *Archiv für Physiologie*, credits these conceptions, which he finds justified by the facts of modern physiology, to Aristotle.

Meanwhile, over against Aristotle and all before and after him who share his mind, still stand Democritus and his successors. If it is a reproach against systematic philosophers that these combatants are unreconciled, it is a reproach against scientists of today, who likewise stand divided and fighting among themselves on the same issue. And the same is true of primitive men wherever they appear and are known to us. There are those who are so immersed in the belief that only matter is real, that their very gods, if they have any gods, are material gods of wood or stones or the sun in the sky. And over against these are the countless multitude of learned and unlearned men who have an indestructible belief in spirit as the most certain reality. There has been never-ending war between these two families of minds, ranging from mutual vituperation to reasoned argument. There has been physical conflict between the two. Men have been put to death for affirming their belief in God. Men have been put to death for declaring there is no God. This war is not over, is never over.

MATERIALISTIC PSYCHOLOGIST VERSUS IDEALISTIC PHYSICIST

In the Sigma Xi *Quarterly* for March, 1939, there appears an article entitled "What Has Become of Reality in Modern Physics?" The author is Professor W. F. G. Swann, director of the Bartol Research Foundation of the Franklin Institute. I notice that Professor Swann was one of the group of fifty men who took part in the symposium on cosmic rays at Chicago in June, 1939. In his article he makes the same journey which Eddington makes from the wooden table of common sense through the atom and electron to whatever may lie beyond. He begins his search for reality where everyone begins. "You will tell me," he writes, "that when you bang your head against the wall, it seems most emphatically evident that there is reality in the wall and that the wall is there."[12] But this experimental physicist looks through the wall to see what it really is. He looks farther and farther and in the end reaches the conclusion that the reality which the physicist seeks is "like the rainbow which seems to descend to the earth at some definite spot but moves away from you as you approach the spot where it seemed to be."[13] His final word is that if you are beguiled into believing that some sorcerer can bring reality to you for inspection you will find in the picture only the image of your own face.

Now one can readily find psychologists who have the conviction that what we used to call

12. p. 33. 13. p. 63.

soul or mind or consciousness-that-does-anything has no reality whatever, and that mind is in reality nothing at all but some kind of organization of activities that go on within the physical brain. Here we have one of the strangest spectacles which the history of mankind affords. Here is a scientific student of mind who has eagerly followed the trail of the scientific students of matter. He believes that he has caught up with them. He believes that the mind which he studies will now and henceforth be known as essentially the same as the matter which the physicist studies. But lo, when this psychologist arrives at this point so long striven for, he finds that Eddington and Swann and others in the forefront of physical research are not at that point any more. They have moved on in their quest for reality and they have arrived at the point which the psychologist abandoned. They have arrived at the conviction that the reality in matter is essentially mind.

Now I, like all the sons of men, belong to a family of minds, and, as in duty bound, I shall state my own belief.

I picture a ladder[14] up which men try to

14. I owe to Plotinus the idea of a ladder whose rounds represent ascending ways of approach toward truth.

climb toward the truth, moved by two irresistible motives—necessity and curiosity. The lowest round of the ladder bears the name of common sense. Most men through all time have gone that high and no higher. Common sense remains a necessity for all men, including the scientist, whether pure or applied. It is most necessary for those scientists who would apply their science to the conduct of human affairs. Without sturdy common sense those scientists who deal with human nature are likely to prove fools. I believe, moreover, that the things and forces which common sense looks upon as real—the wooden table and the strength of the carpenter's arm when he makes the table—do represent realities. But what those underlying realities are common sense does not know. Common sense does not know enough about what is true and does not know well enough what to do. One must leave the lowest round of the ladder and climb higher.

Science as Organized Common Sense

Scientists have climbed higher. Still most of them have said that science is after all just organized common sense. Same kind of facts. Facts known by the same senses. Facts multiplied, measured, organized, when possible mathematically organized. The superior common-sense man can climb the ladder and see what the scientist shows, and the two may join in achieving what are triumphs both of common sense and of science.

Science Transcending Common Sense

But now there is another round in the ladder, which some men of science have climbed in recent decades. Some men eminent in the exact sciences have lately climbed clear and clean up and out of the world which common sense can comprehend and into a world which many scientists in other fields cannot comprehend. These are the supermathematicians, who give us nothing which we can see or picture. They give us formulae which they say represent experimentally verifiable truth and make obsolete much that scientists have hitherto believed true. Whitehead says: "God knows what nonsense will presently be proved true." It isn't simply the man in the street who stands dumb before these unintelligibilities. Most men of science in other fields are equally helpless. A typical attitude of nonmathematical scientists toward the pronouncements of the supermathematicians is that they must doubtless be scientifically valid but have to be accepted as a child accepts the dogmas of the church catechism without a glimpse of understanding. At all events there exists this upper round of the ladder of science, with more and more physicists and mathematicians supporting one another in the belief that they have attained valid scientific results hitherto unknown and inconceivable.

Science and Absolute Truth

What if anything that these men up and down the ladder of science have seen is absolutely true? I do not share the belief of the skeptic toward science who says that the men who have climbed the ladder have seen nothing of which the opposite may not prove equally probable. I do not share the view that science has given us not truth but only gadgets. On the contrary I am so far pragmatist as to believe that if the gadgets work, that is evidence that the science back of them is so far valid. And the gadgets, each more wonderful than the last, with which applied science has filled the world convince me, as they convince most men, that it is a trustworthy approach to the truth of nature—an approach, but not, I believe, final attainment. I share the view of those scientists who regard the so-called laws of nature simply as accounts of the observed behavior of phenomena and never their cause. I accept the report of those who stand upon the highest round of the ladder of science and say that from that round they do not yet see the light which is necessary in order to know the essential nature of any thing, any event, or any act of man.

The Philosophers

But there are those who essay to go higher than the topmost round of the ladder of science. They would go up another round, of which the name is philosophy. I am not of those who abhor or renounce philosophy. Philosophy is a human enterprise which men do not and cannot escape any more than they escape the inevitable urge to win knowledge on any other round of the ladder. A philosophy is a human reaction to the universe. It is impossible that the systematic philosophies should be alike, as it is impossible that the paintings in the galleries of the world should be alike. These diverse systems, these diverse paintings are the expressions of the diverse temperaments of men. Among the great paintings there are certain main types. Among the major philosophies there are families which recur century after century. Thus optimism and pessimism, materialism and idealism do not die out. It is my view that each major type of philosophy is a partial revelation of reality. Of course, being myself one sort of man, I greatly prefer some of these philosophies to others. I especially cherish that gulf stream of philosophies which had its Greek culmination in Plato and Aristotle and which is still, with thousandfold enrichments, moving in the world.

We may think of the beings known to us as a series ascending from what appears most amorphous and inert through all the forms of vegetable and animal life to man and to man in his highest development. All these beings have some characters in common. Each one of them, including the lowest, has within some kind of organization and some kind and amount of resident energy. I share the view also that all things are pervaded by purpose. Within and between all beings there are attractions and repulsions known in part, in part not understood.

But if there are likenesses throughout the series of beings known to us, there are also differences. As we ascend the series we arrive at beings that have life; at beings that have consciousness—first dim, then more and more clear; at beings which contribute relatively more from within to the sum of forces by which their movements are determined; at beings which more and more escape from a small and fixed environment to a larger and changing environment; at beings which more and more select their environments and so determine more and more what forces shall act upon them from without and thus approach free self-determination. But no being known to us has attained complete free self-determination.

The attractions and repulsions within and between beings are very imperfectly understood. Witness the obscurities with regard to intra-atomic attractions and repulsions, and the doubts with regard to gravitation. It is still more difficult to understand rightly the rivalries and coöperations within and between living beings and within and between men. Throughout the universe known to us by common observation, by science and philosophy, there appear likenesses pervading and uniting all things; but also differences, and especially the progressive emergence of order, of life, of consciousness, of determination from within and, at the highest, of a society of persons more and more free and self-determined, united in more and more refined coöperation.

This view of the things known to us strongly indicates the existence of a supreme source of all things—a supreme personal God. I believe that to be the truth. But I believe that what is known through common sense, through science, and through philosophy only indicates and does not demonstrate the existence and character of the Supreme Being—nay, not so much as the innermost nature of the smallest particle of dust—not so much as the real cause of any event whatever.

III

SCHOLAR AND POET

I HAVE pictured a ladder with its lower round occupied by necessary common sense and its higher rounds occupied by organized knowledge in all of its stages up to that which is most exact, most comprehensive, most enlightening, and most useful. Now comes the question: Is there any other way? Is there any way to the discovery of truth which lies beyond the reach of philosophy or of science; that is, beyond the reach of formal logic or of measurements and mathematics?

Many poets and others of like mind say Yes. The Yes of these men is no passing whimsey. It is a conviction that goes in them to the roots of life. On the other hand, many men, learned and unlearned, say No—declare all such claims to be at the best illusory and at the worst fraudulent. So there is a battleground.

Gradgrind and the Poet Who Hate Each Other

Charles Dickens, who was one kind of poet, portrays and caricatures the hardheaded businessman who believes in yardstick, weighing scales, and multiplication table, and nothing else.[1]

> Thomas Gradgrind, sir, is a man of realities, a man of facts and calculations, a man who proceeds upon the principle that two and two are four, and nothing over, and who is not to be talked into allowing for anything over. Thomas Gradgrind, sir—peremptorily Thomas—Thomas Gradgrind. With a rule and a pair of scales and the multiplication table always in his pocket, sir, ready to weigh and measure any parcel of human nature, and tell you exactly what it comes to. It is a mere question of figures, a case of simple arithmetic. You might hope to get some other nonsensical belief into the head of George Gradgrind, or August Gradgrind, or John Gradgrind, or Joseph Gradgrind (all suppositious, nonexistent persons), but into the head of Thomas Gradgrind—no, sir!

The Indispensable Values of Measurements and Mathematics

Dickens was a good hater and a hard fighter against the tribe of Gradgrinds, learned and unlearned. But Thomas Gradgrind does not lack defenders. Foot rule, scale, and the multiplication table, it will be said, are three of

1. *Hard Times,* chapter on "Murdering of Infants."

the most essential discoveries of mankind on the way to civilization. One has only to look at those peoples who have not had those instruments and then at those who have had and used them to see the vital importance of the instruments which Gradgrind so prized. And if one goes beyond Gradgrind to men of science who have used those instruments, one may appraise their value at a yet higher rate. As Millikan says: "Michelson, pure experimentalist, designer of instruments, refiner of techniques, lives because in the field of optics he drove the refinement of measurement to its limits and by so doing showed a skeptical world what far-reaching consequences can follow from that sort of a process and what new vistas of knowledge can be opened up by it."[2]

It is then not surprising that many men of science should agree with Gradgrind that measurements and mathematics have the last word. These men will say that before scientific measurements and mathematics what men had was at best only vague anticipations of the truth. When science comes with its more and more exact scales and its more and more subtle mathematics, the findings of science become the *substitute* for all that men had believed true. Those who have this point of view may

2. *Scientific Monthly,* Jan., 1939.

hold that as exact science goes on its triumphant way, every other supposed way to the truth, and everything else supposed to be true, must surrender step by step until they survive only as specimens in the museums of human archeology.

The subject of these lectures is war. And here certainly is a war that is not yet over, for multitudes of men, including many of the highest eminence, still quite refuse to surrender the belief that there are ways to the truth which lie beyond the reach of formal logic, measurements, and mathematics.

I shall name three groups of men who penetrate the unknown, make discoveries in the unknown, and coöperate successfully with forces which science has not measured and of which science at any date is still ignorant.

All Successful Action Involves Adaptation to Forces Which Are Unmeasured and Unknown to Science

The first group includes everybody in the world whenever they do anything at all. For when a man does anything whatever, he does it within a complex of forces of which he knows some and of which some are unknown to him or to anyone else. When you are asked what you know, you can draw a line and say, this side of the line I know, beyond the line I do not know and have nothing to say. But when you *do* anything you can never draw such a line. The forces that you do not know join with those that you know to determine the results of your action. Germs were here affecting what occurs within every plant and animal millions of years before their existence was suspected by any man. The forces which have been discovered since Galileo were here before Galileo.

For illustration of the difference between answering the question "What is true?" and the question "What shall we do?" consider the physician in charge of a critical case and the experts whom he has called as consultants. We may assume that the consultants represent, at a given date, the best known in the several specialties that touch the case and in the sciences which underlie medicine. They make thorough examinations. They report their findings and then, whatever the date, they must say: "This is as far as our knowledge extends. There are conditions in the case which lie beyond present knowledge. We bid you good bye and wish you well." The physician in charge cannot say that. He must decide what to do. In presence of the known and the unknown conditions, he must act and the patient must take the consequences. All men, learned and unlearned, are essentially in the position of that physician in presence of the known and the unknown universe whenever they must decide what to do.

The human race has survived before and since the advent of science, never by dealing only with that part of the universe which it knew, but also by successful coöperation with the part of the universe which it does not know, a part of the universe which cannot be ignored, which cannot be shut out of effective presence in whatever a man does.

The Expert in Play, Work, or War, Though Often Unlettered, Is a Successful Adventurer and Discoverer of Realities Unknown to Science

All this is most obvious in the second group to which I shall call attention, namely, those men who attain the highest degree of skill in work or play or war. There should be an encyclopedia devoted to the lives and achievements of such men throughout human history. There would be folklore chapters from the past, which few would believe true. There would be accounts of what the most skillful men now do, which few would believe except because they see the things done. There would be accounts of the seeming impossibilities achieved by experts in tennis, golf, billiards, and baseball. There would be accounts of the master technicians in factory and laboratory who in processes where timing is essential have a time sense finer than a split-second watch—a time sense as fine as that of a violinist. There would be chapters on the cook, the Paris chef and the darky mammy who does things in her kitchen as wonderful as he.

Now all these masters of skill are in certain ways alike. What they do is not just luck. It is not just luck when a baseball pitcher puts out twenty-seven batters with eighty-eight thrown balls. It is not just luck when a darky mammy works her kitchen miracles day after day "wid a little dab o' dis an' a little tech o' dat." The master touch does not come by luck, nor is it done by a recipe. The master knows well all that can be seen and stated, but in every master stroke he makes adjustments also to forces which neither he nor anyone else can see or state. Supreme skill is essentially unteachable. The apprentice can look and listen, but he cannot find his way to the master's secret unless and until he also, after bitter travail, is born himself a master.

Consider for an instructive illustration the

history of the curved baseball through the past fifty years. It is a history of continuous new discoveries. There is a succession of men who in their way are supermen—Christy Mathewson, Walter Johnson, "Dizzy" Dean. Some of them are almost illiterate. One and all they are ignorant of what physics has to say of the forces with which they deal. The physicist at any date is ignorant of some of those forces. If he should try to explain those that he does understand, the ballplayer could not understand him any more than the physicist with that knowledge could throw the ball as the pitcher does. But year after year each latest genius finds his way to do a thing with the ball that was never done before and to do it so that the seemingly crazy ball goes time after time exactly where he wills it to go.

Scientific method without doubt leads the way in countless cases to more successful action, but also in countless cases the master of skill discovers the way to successes which the scientist may first declare to be impossible, then acknowledge, then try to explain. A classical instance is the statement of the ranking American mathematician, Simon Newcomb, in 1898, that there never could be an airplane heavier than a watch nor a passenger on such a plane heavier than a mosquito. A few years later the Wright Brothers made such a plane and flew.

The master of a skill is an explorer among unknown forces. He discovers not words but acts, which before his time were impossible to any man, unknown to any man.

Masters of the Fine Arts

I come now to a third group of men who say that their best work, their supreme achievements, were not done by rules laid down by philosophy or by science. These are the artists —the poets, painters, composers of music, and their fellow masters in the fine arts.

There is no lack of science and philosophy relating to what the artist does. There is engineering for the architect. There is anatomy for the sculptor and painter. Physics and physiology unite in sciences of light, color, sound, and tone. There is a science of harmony. There is a science of prosody. There is a science and philosophy of esthetics. Moreover, there are artists who unite scholarship with creative art.

Professor Mosso of the University of Turin has written:

Giotto was painter, sculptor, and architect. Leonardo da Vinci was a celebrated musician, a great painter, an engineer, an architect, a man of letters and of science. Andrea del Verrocchio was goldsmith, sculptor, engraver, architect, painter, and musician. These facts are to be read in many histories of art. An incomparable example, however, is Michelangelo. For twelve years he studied anatomy on the cadaver and afterward painted the Sistine Chapel and executed the Tomb of the Medici and the Dome of St. Peter's.

From such cases one might conclude that the art of these men was simply applied science. Professor Mosso thinks otherwise. He writes: "Even if the genius of these mighty men remains a secret of all time, yet we can see this much, that their hand was just as dextrous as their mind was lofty."[3]

Why should this man of science say that? His own methods as physiologist and psychologist do not remain a secret. Part of what Michelangelo did was no secret. His mechanical engineering was not a secret. The dome as it stands is no secret. Henry Ford could cover the world with copies of it. What was the secret that neither Henry Ford nor any other could discover or copy?

The complete history of St. Peter's is a series of *events* of which the last is the finished

3. *Clark University Decennial Celebration*, p. 387.

work and of which the first was a conception which sometime, somehow came to be within the man Michelangelo. The first event was a conception; the last event was what all the world may see. Now the initial event, the living conception which sometime, somehow came to him, did not come from a blueprint. It did not come from foot rule and scale. It was not a recipe from any sort of scholarship. It is the first essential event within the man whom we call Michelangelo whose source, Mosso says, must remain a secret for all time.

It may be that supreme human achievements of every sort have their beginnings in some such initial conception within a man whom we call a genius. Julian Huxley says that one of Darwin's greatest discoveries came to him as "a revelation." Darwin himself writes: "I can remember the very spot in the road whilst in my carriage when, to my joy, the solution occurred to me." Helmholtz reports a similar experience when he was on vacation in the high Alps. Such essential initial events within a man of genius, leading to a supreme achievement, are doubtless among the most important events in the history of men on the earth. Scientist and philosopher may try to account for these essential events, each in his own way. To the man who experiences them, they are inexplicable. They come like the wind which bloweth where it listeth and thou canst not tell whence it cometh nor whither it goeth. If that be mysticism, Mr. Thomas Gradgrind, something like it was known not only to Michelangelo but also to Helmholtz and to Darwin.

But if Michelangelo's science could not teach him the secret of his art nor reveal that secret to others, how was it with Homer? There was nothing that we call science known to Homer or to his Hellenes when they fought at Troy and "burned the topless towers of Ilium." It was not Aristotle, chief justice among those who announced the laws of poetry—it was not Aristotle who taught the Greek poets how to sing. Homer, Aeschylus, Sophocles, Pindar, Sappho all died before Aristotle was born. He did not teach them. They taught him all that he knew of the art of the poet.

The living things on the earth have a common origin and have essential elements in common, but have also in their evolution grown to be far apart—in organs and functions, in processes and products. In a group of beings such as men there appear such essential kinships and such profound divergences as, for example, in the white, black, red, and yellow races. Now the processes involved in the production of works of science and of art are life processes occurring within men; and like all other life processes they have essential elements in common and have developed along divergent paths.

A finding of science and a work of art are alike in origin. They are alike in the test of their truth and worth.

The origin of each finding of science and of each work of art is the experience of a man. Scientist and artist alike fare forth through the universe which all of us inhabit. Each of them in his adventure touches and is touched, selects and reacts, according to his inherited and acquired constitution; and each brings forth in his own language a report of what he has lived through.

Their languages are far apart. The scientist reports his experience in a statement, perhaps in a formula. The artist's report of his experience is in some kind of music, music of words, music of tone, music of color, music of form. Their languages are so far apart that none of them can be rightly translated into any of the others. Each man speaks in his own tongue. Long ago in Berlin I heard Paulsen say: To understand a language is to feel its untranslatability. Far apart are the languages, but all at their best speak truth—tell with scrupulous veracity what something in the universe has said to a man.

The test of truth and worth is the same for scientist and for artist. The supreme test for what each man reports is the judgment of those who come nearest to sharing his experience. No human judgment, indeed, is infallible. Each rising genius, whether artist or scientist, must meet the misjudgments not only of the uninstructed multitude but also often the adverse judgments of eminent old men whose work his own discredits. It was physicians who fought Pasteur. It was musicians who fought Wagner. It was Voltaire, pontiff of literature, who, speaking before the high court of the French Academy a century and a half after the death of Shakespeare, denounced Shakespeare as a menace to the theater and to art. Time remedies many such misjudgments—doubtless not all of them. In the end Pasteur and Wagner were victors. In the end, as Heine says, the kings of literature elected Shakespeare emperor.

Nevertheless, the best judgment we have upon the work of any man is always the judgment of those who come nearest to sharing his experience—never the judgment of friend or foe who is alien to his experience. The supreme court before which Newton and Einstein must stand does not include Boone or Lincoln or Shelley or Wagner or the Apostle Paul. That court must be composed of fellow supermathematicians. So neither can the supreme court for the judgment of Shakespeare or Beethoven or any artist in whatever art be made up of metaphysicians, psychologists, or others, however eminent in some other world than the world of art. The supreme court for the poet can be made only of men who themselves have known the agony and joy of the creative artist.

Scientist and artist look at whatever they will anywhere in the universe. Both look at nature. One comes with news of atoms or stars or the living things on our earth. The other comes with a nature song of Theocritus, or the pastoral symphony of Beethoven. Both look at human nature. One comes with his sociology, his economics, his psychology. The other comes with his painting, his novel, his drama. Each man has the advantage of his method. Each suffers the limitations of his method. If it is atoms or stars or molecules or genes, if it is something which can be seen with telescope or microscope, something which can be counted or measured, then it is the scientist who can bring us the most news of it. From such come the great and always greater triumphs of science. But always there are realities which at any date lie beyond the methods and instruments of science. Those realities which lie farthest beyond the reach of measuring and counting are the deeps of human behavior. Then it is not Galileo with his telescope, nor any son of Galileo with any more cunning instrument, who sees farthest into this reality. It is Shakespeare or it is Beethoven, or it is other artists who approach their vision, who know, as no scholar can know, what men are and what they do at the best and at the worst.

In 1610, Galileo saw the moons of Jupiter, an epoch-making event which, says Einstein, marks the beginning of science as now understood. That same year, Shakespeare saw Caliban and his mother, that damned witch Sycorax. What, if anything real, did Shakespeare then see?

Not in the vexed Bermoothes, but in Stratford and in London Shakespeare saw, as only some kind of poet can see, the deeps that are in man. He saw what men want, what they fight for. He saw those in whom the lower hungers that belong within a man are victorious, in whom the higher hungers that belong within a man are choked, smothered, dying, or dead. He saw, at the worst, those in whom the sight of health and happiness and innocence and joy is a torture. He saw these things, not as abstractions, not as formulae. He saw them where alone they exist—in living personalities, Edmund, Prince John, Iago. It is not Aristotle, nor Hegel, nor Freud, nor any psychologist—it is only Shakespeare, or such as he, who knows the reality that is Iago.

There are many dramatists, novelists, painters, composers who see the worst of men, as Shakespeare did, and some of them, including some of the very great, see nothing else. Thomas Hardy says that, in mercy, the evolution of life should have stopped with the mollusk. Above the mollusk there is the continuation of the same tragedy, and with it pain and no hope. Some would write over the gates of life what Dante saw over the gate of his Inferno: "Abandon hope all ye who enter here." But there are poets who bring from the deeps of their experience another report. Goethe lived from youth to age with his Faust. He knew the fearful commerce of Faust with the powers of darkness. But through the years Goethe knew that there is something in man which Hell cannot hold. And Dante, who in the men and women of his Florence saw all the descending circles of his Inferno, had also another sight. He saw the multitude who will not abandon hope; who, under every circumstance that invites despair and surrender, do not despair and will not surrender. That is, he saw the Purgatory whose folk have the indestructible will toward the inner goodness and the inner blessedness which are Paradise.

It is written: "All things flow; nothing abides." Men of science have been made to realize this in our time perhaps as never before because of the rapidity with which our most certain conceptions give way to others. The flights of our present-day physicists from the seeming solid ground of common sense in search of a more solid reality recall Eliza's flight across the Ohio on floating blocks of ice. She left the ground of Kentucky for what seemed a safe island of solid ice, but then was forced to leap from one insecure block to the next and to the next. Eliza, in the story, arrived at last on a shore as solid as Kentucky. Where do the fleeing physicists of our day arrive? They do not agree. Some of the foremost of them have fallen into skepticism of science even as Pyrrho and Pascal. For them there is no solid shore anywhere, but only floating, frozen blocks that melt on their way to an unknown sea. But most men of science surrender to no such skepticism. They do, indeed, realize that all things and all formulae are transient and that, as it was written of old, all things flow. But they find everywhere within the flow evidence of indwelling order, of which all men have a glimpse and of which men, at the best, see more and more. They see science as a stream whose past is the history of science, whose present is the front wave of one part of the cosmic evolution.

Science is a river. When it seems most solid, it is in flow. As it flows in the minds of men of science it is a partial revelation, and we believe an always fuller revelation of what is in reality true. Science is one form of the ever-living cosmic evolution, but not the only form in which the underlying reality touches the minds of men. Reality, whatever it is, touches every man, gives every man some bits of experience which at least enable him to keep alive. And the underlying reality pours itself in flood through the poets, painters, musicians, seers, and in forms of beauty gives to them and to us the most deep and most certain revelations of truth which are possible for men. All things that men have made are mortal. But of all the things that men have made on earth, those which have endured longest in the very forms in which they were born are the supreme works of art.

The poet—whatever his art—stands always in the midst of the doctors—doctors of theology, of philosophy, of science, and now of psychology. The doctors look at the poet. They say what they will of him. That is their right. That is their vocation. What the wisest doctors say of the poet has high value. What the less wise (friends or foes) say of him ranges down and down to worthlessness or worse.

The scholar has traveled far through many realms, but not everywhere. He has much to tell, but not everything. The poet also has traveled—through realms which lie beyond the reach of the instruments and logic of the scholar. When he tells what he has seen he cites no book of learning. The master poet—in whatever art—speaks as one having authority, the authority of his own intercourse with Reality.

Autobiographical

I have traveled among strange men—men of the countryside, men in the street, scientists, metaphysicians, poets, seers—men who in their extreme differences are as far apart as the white, black, red, and yellow races. An anthropologist, student of a race, goes to live with its people, tries to understand them as nearly as possible as they understand themselves. Then only does he undertake to judge the worth of their ways of life. I know how far it is beyond me to know the diverse families of minds as the races of mankind are known to the anthropologist. But I share his spirit. In my journeys of fifty years among men whose beliefs and ways are remote from mine, I have tried so far as possible to see the world through their eyes. But I have also looked at the world through my own eyes. I have not been (as Bourget says of Renan) one who would savor many beliefs and possess none. And this is the chief of what I have seen. I have had sight of chaos and hell, but also, on every side, I have seen the irrepressible emergence of order, reason, beauty, love.

INDEX